Praise for *One Giant Psychological Leap for Humankind*

D1277716

I first met Dr. Dale in graduate school. I soon realized that he was the most sympathetic, decent and brilliant man I had ever met. His book is reflective of the man I have known all these years. I recommend that anyone interested in human value read the book.
Alan Chartock, Ph.D.
CEO, WAMC Northeast Radio
Professor Emeritus, State University of New York

With imaginative, innovative, and ingenious writing, Dr. Jan Dale introduces readers to intriguing relationship skills for positive parenting and loving marriages that potentially could be "One Giant Psychological Leap for Humankind." Rooted in Rogerian psychological theory, but enhanced by Dale's own intellectual insights, this breakthrough book demonstrates how he practices what he professes, both in his own personal life and professional counseling.
Donald E. Messer, Ph.D., Executive Director,
Center for Health and Hope, Denver, CO;
President Emeritus, Iliff School of Theology, Denver, CO

This book is a distillation of Jan's forty years of experience as a practicing psychologist. The book reflects Jan's humanity, his optimism, and his belief that loving, sensitive parents can do much to launch their children on the road to happy, meaningful lives.

With humor and numerous real life examples, Jan demonstrates the importance of skill training in communication and conflict resolution throughout the life cycle. His insights and down-to-earth advice will be useful to all who aspire to be better parents and better partners.

Carole Kazmierski, Ph.D.
Psychologist in Private Practice, Minneapolis, MN

Dr. Jan Dale offers a challenging "third alternative", as we consider how we want to relate to our children, our mates, and our global partners. Rather than being passive or authoritarian, we are encouraged to enhance our active listening skills, and seek creative approaches to conflict resolution thereby nurturing persons who are self-confident, empathic, and caring of others.

Bonnie Messer, Ph.D.
Pscyhologist in Private Practice, Denver, CO

One Giant Psychological Leap for Humankind

A Future of Healthy Kids, Healthy Adults, Healthy Religions, and Healthy Countries

by Jan Dale

Family Success
Press
www.familysuccesspress.com

Family Success Press
3320 Dartmoor LN
Ames IA 50014
USA
www.familysuccesspress.com
editor@familysuccesspress.com

Family Success
Press
www.familysuccesspress.com

ONE GIANT PSYCHOLOGICAL LEAP FOR HUMANKIND: A
FUTURE OF HEALTHY KIDS, HEALTHY ADULTS, HEALTHY
RELIGIONS, AND HEALTHY COUNTRIES:

ISBN-13:   978-0-9848942-3-9

ISBN-10:   0-9848942-3-3

Cover design and interior layout © 2016 by polytekton.com

Dedicated to my wife of fifty-three years, Donna—always there for me—and my precious kids, Kristin, Jeff, and Jon—all of whom were pure joy to raise—and my gold mine, my grandkids, Jaden, Sofia, Ty, Elliot, Grace, and Lucia. I'm privileged to be your grandpa. It's so much fun to watch you grow.

Table of Contents

Preface

The subject of this book is how normal people can acquire happy and fulfilled lives. The author describes the very best of a life in every stage and shows the relationship skills that make it happen.

The ultimate purpose of the book is to encourage society to include psychological skill training in schools, colleges, churches and communities in order to maximize successful relationships. Skilled individuals make for healthy parents who can then produce healthy and happy children. The author's argument here is that human life can be greatly improved, thereby preventing the tragedy and unhappiness we see today in so many normal families.

Childless couples may not need the parenting skills of this book since they don't have children to raise but they may have close relationships to nieces and nephews or neighbors and friends. Or perhaps they work with children. Childless couples may certainly be interested in the adult love relationship skills presented here. Similarly, the book emphasizes couples, but the single parent will benefit from the parenting skills. And since the single parent is not married he or she may still have a love relationship where the relationship skills would be helpful.

This book is timely, as the United States Congress is motivated at this time to find money and solutions to prevent mass shootings. Society has the professionals now who have the kind of skills the author presents in this book. Society just needs a lot more of these professionals. The county in west Chicago that has the highest current random murder rate in

2016 has instituted parent training as one of its attempts to stop violence. We need to get full time mental health professionals into prevention where they can do skill training and not just remedial treatment. We need more mental health professionals for skill training for prevention and we need more mental health professionals for treatment for the underserved and less accessible areas of the country.

The United States Appropriation Bill for 2017 (FY2017) calls for prevention and has ample funding to easily train a new cadre of mental health professionals. Innovations in the United States are very often followed up and set into motion by many other countries. This could be the beginning of a giant psychological leap forward for humankind. This book demonstrates the positive results that could come from such skill training of normal people.

I want to thank all those who helped me write this book. First, I want to thank my wife Donna who proofread my book and who has helped me in all things in life. My daughter Kristin proofread as well. I must thank all my children, Kristin, Jeff, and Jon, through whom I could prove the veracity of psychological skills for parenting of all stages.

I need to thank my friend and fellow writer, Joe Geha, long time professor of writing at Iowa State University, who went over my book with a fine tooth comb. Another important person who proof read my book, and advised me on the perspectives of women, was my long time private practice partner, Dr. Carole Kazmierski.

And finally a special thanks to my copy editor, Dr. Mary Fry Liebich, who worked diligently to give rapid birth to this book in spite of her demanding teaching schedule.

Introduction

This book has three voices: Dan, (narrating all the stages of his life), Dan's psychologist Grandpa, (who gives backdrop perspective to Dan's journey), and Jan, the author, (who later in the book presents a model for successful relationships.)

The story is about two neighbor boys who stay connected all through their lives, Dan and Charles. Dan had the good fortune of being born to parents and grandparents who already knew the very best ways to care for, and to love, a child. These parents and grandparents had skill training. Charles' parents did not.

I'm going to show the differences in their lives, throughout all the stages of their lives. I'm going to show how the two sets of parents handled their kids, and how all the stages of the kids' lives went. (In this book, I'm talking about healthy psychological parenting, and how it results in healthy development of children. I do recognize that children with genetic mental illnesses, or children with brain damage can be born into the healthiest of parenting and yet have grave struggles. But the skills presented here can help those families cope as well.)

With your permission, I'm going to take the privilege of speaking through my characters. So even though they are doing the talking in the pages to come it is me you hear coming through their voices – hopefully you will notice that much of the time Dan sounds wise beyond his years.

Have you ever heard a fetus, a day old child, or a one-year-old, speak with such authority to the people of the world? Well, you are hearing them now. This is my psychological description of what a fetus, an infant, a toddler, an elementary aged child, a preteen and a teenager might be feeling about his or her psychological environment. This is portrayed in the voice of Dan through all these stages.

The voice of Dan describes all the stages of life including terminal stages and facing death. His voice is interlaced with his psychologist grandfather's commentary and toward the end the author, my own voice, describes the skills to make the happy and fulfilled life that results from people having psychological skills in their relationships.

I think kids do know what is right for them, and good for them, even though they may not have the language to say it. With your permission I'm going to give them the language. Let's get started. Dan is soon to be born.

One Giant Psychological Leap for Humankind

(Dan:) Thump. Thump. Thump. Thump. That sound is so reassuring. It is always there. My mother's heart is beating right up there above me. I don't know what it is, but I like it.

It gives me a feeling of consistency. I'm not aware yet that she is there for it will be a few more weeks until everything changes and I learn about her. But for now, it's just simply nice. For now I have no worries really. I have no hunger yet because I must be fed in some totally miraculous way.

What I know for now is just a really smooth thing. I'm swimming much of the time. My limbs move quite often and it's so much fun to feel my muscles working. My thumb even ends up in my mouth sometimes and I suck away when that happens. I enjoy the sloshing around in this water with a perfect temperature. It's soothing and relaxing. If I knew there were other people and that we all started out in nine months of this, I'd say all people have a good beginning filled with peace, happiness, the freedom to move and a feeling of being loved, like all is good.

What a great world I have here. It's the only world I know. I'm not sure exactly when I first came to be, but it happened some time ago. All of a sudden I was here and here I am. I like it. Sometimes besides that great thump, thump, thump, there is a higher pitched sound. It starts and stops. Sometimes it's louder and sometimes quite soft. But whenever it happens, I like it. It's part of my world. At this point I have no idea it's my mother's voice. All I know for now is that I like it. It comes and it goes. It's interesting. It's soothing.

I have no idea why I'm here. I have no memory of anything before this. I have no reason to think anything else would ever occur other than this. I'm just here and I like it. I don't really know what trust and safety is. I don't know what love is. All I can express is that I like this life. It's good. I'm glad I'm here.

Now I'm Born

(Dan:) Whoa! Whoa! What was that? It seems like something happened to that wonderful water. It has been surrounding me for my entire life. I thought it was forever. Why would it whoosh away all of a sudden, allowing some kind of collapsing of my world around me? It feels as if I have fallen somewhat. I'm up against something I've not known before. It's not really hard but I don't like it. This is different. For the first time in my life I feel discomfort. This isn't right. For the first time in my life I feel unsafe. This I do not trust. This is different and for the first time something isn't right and it isn't good. I don't like it. There is an uneasy feeling in my stomach that I've never felt before. It will be years before I will know this as nervousness, fear and anxiety, but for now it's new to my world, something I didn't know of before and I wish I could go back. If there is a creator of all this, why would that creator create this bad stuff?

Ouch! What the...!! Now what? I don't like this either, but something is pushing my hind end. It's shoving my head right up against a wall. I wish it would stop and let me go back. But it only seems to get worse. What a load of pressure on a little fellow. Why am I being shoved so rudely? Am I not alone in this world? What's shoving me? I wish it would stop it.

Oh my God! I'm not up against a wall at all. It's started to give. My head is moving into something soft but tight. Whatever else is in this world but me must be mean spirited. This isn't good and it's not right. I did nothing to deserve this. I thought the world I lived in was trustworthy, dependable and forever giving and nice. This isn't nice. And it's not fair.

By now my head is stuck. And so far there seems to be no turning back, although I wish there were. I'd hate to spend a second lifetime with my head stuck. What happened to all the fun I've enjoyed for so long?

What happened to the calm soothing sloshing around? My muscles always felt so good. I swam like an Olympic medal winner with no contest whatsoever. I ruled. I dominated. I was the king of the world. What's this crap? Where's the bad force coming from, what is it up to, and what has happened to my happy world? Frankly if I knew the word for it, I would be scared to death. Maybe my life wasn't to be forever in a calm ecstatic bliss. But if not, why did it start out soooooo nice? If it wasn't always to be nice, why did it start so nice?

If there's another being in my world that made me and gave me that wonderful start, what the heck is it doing to me now and why? Am I bad? I'm sure being mistreated now. Was I made to be mistreated? I'm not looking forward to what happens next, I can tell you. The feeling of trust and safety that I had for so long has turned in a second to mistrust and fear. What could happen to me next? This hurts. Am I being moved into a world of pain like this? I don't want it. I want what I had. But I have a sinking feeling there is no turning back. My sweet world is leaving me and I have no idea what's going to happen to me next. I thought there were only one life and one world. I was the king of the world. I ruled supreme. All my needs were met while I just hung out and goofed off, swimming, exercising, and basking in the warm bath.

Apparently the nice world is gone. I still have life, but my life no longer feels good. It's not trustworthy. I could be hurt. I am being hurt. Now my shoulders have been shoved into this tunnel with my head and I don't like it. I'm stuck. I'm trapped. Something's got a firm hold on the top of my body, which used to be so free. If I knew the word crushed, I would be turning to it now to try to explain to myself and to others what the heck is happening. This can't be good. And for how long will this go on? Forever? Forget it. I don't want this life. This is no kind of a life.

This is a huge squeeze. A good hug would be one thing, but this goes above and beyond the call of duty. Please leave me be and stop this big squeezing thing.

I even lost the sound of the heartbeat. I hear no comforting voice above me. All is dead quiet in here. There is nothing to reassure me. Whoops. Here I go again. I'll be darned if my hips are now caught in this as well. The only movement that I can express is in my legs and feet, and they, too, are getting more confined. Ah, now, even they are caught and stuck. My whole body is stuck. This is ugly. I don't like it. I always felt so good shooting my arms and legs around, catching my thumb in my mouth. If I knew the word freedom yet, I would have said it is essential to human beings – if I knew there were other human beings. All that moving around was so nice. I loved it. When I slept, I might just spread out and enjoy the jostling around of the water, while I trustingly just floated in utter safety. I slept like a log. Or some might say, I slept like a baby. My mother would have said: He's quiet now. Nothing is happening. And we were good.

What the…? Something hard has come in here from the front of this squeeze tunnel and grabbed me by the head. Ouch. Stop it. It's grabbed hold onto both sides of my head. And now it's pulling me. What the….?

I'm slipping again. Everything's started to move now. Something's pulling me by my head. That's inconsiderate. Couldn't you grab a hold of something other than my head? This apparently is another world now as I keep slipping along. A world of head grabbers, I suppose. I don't like the way they treat people here. This can't be good.

Oh my gosh, it's bright. And it's loud. But most of all, it's colder than anything I can imagine. I'm cold and wet in a bright environment of big creatures. They have on masks. There are nothing but eyes staring over masks. What a way to greet a fellow. No faces. Wait, there's a face back there on that bed. And fortunately the eyes are warm, happy, even loving, but she's crying. No, wait a minute. She's smiling and laughing. No, I was wrong again. She's crying. Huh, she's doing both.

Oh great, now this big creature behind the mask is holding me upside down. Is that any way to greet a newcomer to this world? I'm going to give him a piece of my mind now. He'll regret doing this to me. Oh no, besides holding me upside down, now he's starting to beat me on my butt. Somebody stop this guy.

He's totally out of control and inappropriate. If only I were bigger. Oh well. I'm not. But I've had it. Hold on everyone. You are going to witness one powerful little king of his world show his stuff. I'm going to yell now. He'll be sorry. And they all will. Maybe I can make them scared for a change. All except that nice one with the warm and happy eyes who can't seem to decide if she's happy or sad. She's all right, but the rest of them must be sadists. I think they are enjoying this. They seem to support what he's doing. Ok here it comes. And with that, I just started yelling at the top of my voice, or since I am upside down, at the bottom of my body. There. That'll teach them.

What the heck something is happening to my chest? It's heaving up and down. I'm gasping. He's got his rubber fingers in my face. He's sticking something in my nose, and now the air is flowing in and out of my lungs. Hmmm. This is kind of interesting. It just keeps up. In and out. In and out. It doesn't seem to be stopping. In and out. What's this about? I never did this, in where I was. But I'm still doing it.

Hey. The sadist stopped hitting me. And he turned me over. Why would he do a kind thing like that? He's tucked me in close. Now he handed me to another person and she tucked me in close. She is wrapping me in something really soft and nice. Now this is more like it. Are they going to stop mistreating me all of a sudden? Apparently they think I've had enough mistreatment. Thank God.

Oh Good. Besides wrapping me up nicely and getting me warm again, she's handing me to the warm eyed one. She isn't crying anymore. She's just smiling. Wait. Don't unwrap me. Here comes the cold again. Oh great. You make a little progress, and they take it away. I'm freezing again. Wait, they are putting me on the chest and stomach of the nice one. Whoa. What a soft and warm chest! Now she's wrapping me up again on my back and putting a soft warm hand down around my bottom. That feels good. She is gentle. She seems to be holding me close, like I'm valuable again, or something.

Whoops, she put her lips on my head. Now her lips are on my cheek. I think I'm going to be all right. I hope she's the one to keep me rather than the big one with the hard instrument that he used on my head. I think he's gone now. Good. I hope I don't see him again. I'll stay with this nice one here, if you don't mind. I think I like her.

There she did it again. She put her lips on my head again. She's nice, I believe. She's not going to hurt me, and I don't think she'd let anyone else hurt me. This is good. Now what? That second one who held me has her finger in my mouth. Now what's she up to?

Well, look at me. I'm sucking the heck out of her finger just because she stuck it in my mouth and moved it around a few times. Would you believe it? Now she's taking it away, just when I was starting to enjoy sucking it. What kind of a capricious world is this? Can you depend on anything nice lasting? Just as I am mistrusting, this nice warm eyed smiling one has put something from her warm chest in my mouth too.

This chest thing is not so bony like the nurse's finger and it's warmer, bigger, and considerably softer. Actually, its' quite a mouth full, if you want to know.

But what now? I'm sucking again like mad, not knowing for sure why, and now my stomach is warm. Boy is this good. This is delicious. I've never tasted anything before, but this is good. I think I'll just keep on sucking if no one minds. More and more are leaving the room. It's just mostly me and the nice one, and do I love this warm stomach feeling. I never got to do this before. Maybe this world is going to be OK after all and you know what, it's interesting to get to suck like this, and get something from it. I like this. And now she's rubbing my little back. She just counted my toes. Now she's checking out my long fingernails. What the heck. She just put her lips to my fingernails!

Maybe I'm going to be the king of this world too. What a relief. This is a nice place. In my previous life I had no idea that this world was here in addition to my first world. There was no way I could know. I guess my trust and safety feelings should have told me if there would be another world than the one I know, it, too, would be good, trustworthy and safe. One thing I have learned already is that if I ever get shoved out of this new world, I won't have to fear there not being another. If someone nice were here to receive me and take care of me this time, wouldn't it be true another time as well? I think I'll go to sleep. It's been a big day. Good night for now. In some ways, even though this new world is scarier than the old, it's starting to seem a little more interesting. I wonder what tomorrow will bring in this new world? Will I be safe? Talk to you later.

Well, it's been two or three days now in this new world. I mostly like it. The one with the warm eyes and soft and delicious chest seems to stay around me the most. She isn't crying anymore. She just seems to smile all the time, both at me and anyone else who comes to visit. Some guy has shown up a lot too, and he holds me quite a bit. I'm starting to like him, but he's not got the great chest, for some reason, like this warm eyed one. And he's harder. But he's always smiling like the warm eyed one. They are easy to be around. They laugh a lot. I think I'm going to like them both.

Coming Home

(Dan:) I am going for my first ride today but I can't see a whole lot. They have me wrapped up in this tight chair of some kind and left a cover over me most of the time. I didn't mind that because it is cozy in here. But I'm not going to learn a lot with my head covered up all the time. Whatever world is outside this car I sure as heck can't see it. I hope they leave the cover off sometimes, because I'd like to know more about this new world.

We are entering this house. Now they are setting my chair down. They take the cover off and here I am in a nursery all decked out with colors all around. They lay me in a bed with something that moves above my head. It's interesting. Whoops, I'm getting tired as I watch it and here I am falling to sleep again. They are both up there, looking down smiling. Why are they so happy all the time? Good night.

The days pass now. I get the delicious soft chest about every three hours they say, night and day, which is a good deal. Sometimes just before I get it, I'll yell because my stomach hurts. The nice thing is that my yelling brings them right away. My stomach never hurts very long. That's good.

I sleep a lot these days. It's a lot like my former world in that sense. I think I slept quite a bit there too. I feel the best, when one of these two that I live with, holds me. I feel really secure, trusting and happy when they hold me. If they set me down too soon after I eat, during the night, I'll yell until they pick me up and hold me some more.

I like to be around them when I'm awake. It's interesting to see what they are doing and to learn about this world. Sometimes really small people will visit our house and they intrigue me to no end. They will come up and look right into my eyes. One very tiny one, got close, smiled, and I was happy, then she poked her finger toward my eye and just missed it. Most of the big people were upset with her. The bigger kids seem safer than she does. I'll kind of be a little nervous when she gets close. The warmed-eyed one, or the harder chest guy, stay close when she visits now. And I've not got the finger again, so far.

In these early weeks and months, my stomach will get kind of off, and I'll whine when that happens. I can see that always worries the two I live with. They kind of frown and worry at those times and try their best to come up with something to entertain me. If I hear a really loud noise that upsets me, and scares me, I always yell and cry until they hold me a while, then I get to feeling safe again.

I'm sure glad she comes with the warm and soft chest during the nights, as well as the days. I can tell it's hard for her to do. I think she wants to sleep longer, but she's always nice to me anyway, and I get the delicious feeling in my stomach when she's there. Although sometimes my stomach gets off and I fuss even at night and they worry, but don't seem to blame me, or anything. I've heard them say "when he's three months he'll sleep through, and his digestive system will mature, and then it will be easier for us." But, of course, I didn't know what this meant, because I don't understand language, yet. But just saying it seemed to make them both feel better. I can tell they don't want my stomach to hurt, and they always try to entertain me or help me get to sleep when it hurts, even if it's in the middle of the night. They are pretty nice. I think I am really liking them. They make this new scary world, with pain and all, much easier to handle. I sure wouldn't want to be without them, I can tell you that. I wonder if there is a creator of this life, and world, who cares when we suffer, like these two seem to care? Why else would a good creator allow for a hard side of life?

After having my hands and legs always flailing around in my life, all of a sudden I'm able to control them. I can reach out for things and feel them. First thing I do, is pull them into my mouth, to see what they taste like. I'm trying to hold and taste the world as much as possible these days. I turn things over and over after I taste them. All these objects around me are so interesting. Get your hands, faces, or glasses near me, and I'll twist and turn them straight into my mouth if I can.

Sometimes people pull their glasses back. Those things are the hardest to get a good reading, as to what they are like, and how they feel. Wonder why people are so touchy about those things anyway? As far as I can tell, the soft chested one's father is the only one, who will let me maul his glasses. Good thing I have him. I know now what his glasses taste and feel like, but his are the only ones so far. There isn't much he won't let me explore. Sometimes the others get upset with him for letting me touch most anything. But he just smiles and usually lets me do it, in his house anyway. I'm really starting to be with him as much as possible. He can be with me about as long as I wish. He lets me stand and jump on his lap a lot too. That came along right after the grabbing and holding things. All of a sudden when I push my legs, I go up. He laughs and I laugh.

I'm glad to say the masked up guy with the hard clamps that pulled me into this world hasn't been seen since. I'm happy with it that way. Because he wasn't too nice, and I sure could have used someone kinder to welcome me out of that tight tunnel into this place. I wish the warm eyed one with the soft chest, or this other guy with the hard chest, could have pulled me out. They wouldn't have grabbed my head like that I just know they wouldn't have.

But unfortunately, there's another guy somewhat like the masked up guy who lives in an office downtown. We drive there, which is fun, but as soon as I see his office, I start to let them know I'm not interested. They lovingly but firmly disregard my protests, and take me to him anyway. But fortunately they don't leave me there, and I know they wouldn't, because they like me for sure. But I'm a little confused as to why they keep taking me back there. And they always seem kind of excited when we go there. They look proud and happy while he pokes my stomach and looks in my mouth. That's not so bad. I don't mind that. But occasionally he brings out a sharp thing, and for no particular reason, he sticks me in the butt or in the arm. It's not fair. And it's not good.

The warmed eyed one always looks really hurt too, when I yell, and she grabs me right after and holds me tightly against her warm chest, and lets me look over her shoulder, away from the painful guy. The pain doesn't last long each time, so I've come to know that much. But that's about my only question about them, namely, why they seem so happy each time we go there, and why they keep taking me so often. When I learn to talk, I'll give them a piece of my mind about it and find out what the heck he's doing in our lives. Without him, it would all be pretty good, except for that little girl who sticks fingers in eyes. We could do without her too.

Finally I'm Past Three Months

(Dan:) Well, I guess we're past three months because I heard them announce that one day, although I didn't know what it meant, of course. But I've noticed my stomach feels good all the time now, and I'm sleeping all night long, which they seem to be ecstatic about. It doesn't make a whole lot of difference to me. I enjoyed their attention at night. But they don't look so dark around the eyes anymore, which I just figured was the way they looked. And I know they are happy with my sleeping when it's dark. But it was fun to be with them during the nights, which doesn't happen anymore, unless I throw up or have a bad dream. Then fortunately, they come running in.

If ever I cry or yell or get scared, they come to me. They pick me up and hold me to their soft and hard chests, and then I feel better. They do a good job of keeping me feeling safe. I trust them. I actually trust everyone but that one in the office downtown because everyone else smiles at me; they touch my cheek, and say things like "he's so cute." So I trust everyone because these two I live with are trustworthy. I hear these two say some other kids "don't feel trusting and safe because their parents aren't so devoted to their every need" like mine are, and that these kids are angry and nervous all the time. Of course, I couldn't understand what they said. But it seemed important to them.

One of the things I love the most is when people get down and hold their faces fairly close to mine. I've always loved looking at faces for some reason. Remember, when I was born,

I picked up on the warm eyed person in the bed right from the start. I also was watching the eyes peer over those masks too. I don't know what it is about eyes, but I've always stared at eyes. It still remains one of my favorite things to do.

Maybe I'm trying to figure out people when I study their eyes. I know I love to just stare up at the warm eyed one's eyes, while I lay at her chest, sucking as if there was no tomorrow. She seems to enjoy staring back when we do that and I just feel good all over.

But anyone else can bring the same kind of strong interest, if he or she gets down in my face and stares and smiles. I can stare back all day if the person wants to stay. Her face is so interesting to me. And I feel like a million bucks when she is down that close. I often bat my eyes and smile and she will smile back. Sometimes she will talk in a high voice which I also adore. If she'll touch my cheek I'll smile for sure, and wrinkle my nose, just out of some happiness to have her down here staring at me.

It sure beats having people across the room engaged in adult conversation with someone else while I go unnoticed, or busy getting a meal, or doing something else that's important in their world. Sometimes I am content just exploring toys by myself, or jumping in my jumper, or lying under toys that hang from above me, while I kick my feet and wave my hands in the air. But if I just get some of this close face time, I'm pretty excited and happy, because for some reason, I love it.

My parents have never dropped me once or let me fall off the changing table or down the steps. But they seem to fear it might happen sometime even though they try their best to avoid such things. I'm even not afraid when the hard chested one throws me up over his head. In fact, I love it. By the time I'm coming down, I'm laughing almost uncontrollably, I love it so much. And I'm old enough now that I can make my legs kind of jump a little bit on his lap when he's just done it so he'll know I want to do it again. And most of the time when I jump like that, he will do it again. In fact, he does it quite a few times which I just love. I just laugh, and laugh, and laugh. The only way he can get me to stop jumping is by bringing something else interesting up in front of my face to get me interested in something else. Otherwise, I'd do it all day.

The nice thing about him is that when he does it, I always feel safe. He doesn't do it too wild or rough. I've had a few big guys, on what they called family reunions, who got some kind of bang out of tossing me up pretty hard and scary. Yes, I was still laughing uncontrollably, but I was really scared and wished they'd stop. I had no control over when they would stop, and they paid no attention to the fear in my eyes, since I was laughing out of control. I feel sorry for their children. I'll bet their children won't grow up with a sense of physical safety like me, nor will they be as inclined to grow on into competitive sports like I will, because I trust contact. It's fun for me because my hard chested parent is always gentle with his rough housing, never overly scary, or rough. So I can let myself be physical and enjoy it.

(Grandpa:) Overly aggressive roughhousing parents will wonder why their little children may cower from sports and not want to get physical. Their sons will learn from what these rough parents do that it's an unsafe arena of life. Usually this is exactly the opposite thing these parents want. They want their kids to enjoy and excel in athletics. They can end up sorely disappointed and be critical of their children not knowing that they themselves created the condition that turned their kids away from sports. These parents think by tossing their kids high, even though they squeal from fear, that their children will become rough and tough and aggressive at sports. The exact opposite can be true.

It seems to me two trends have been growing in sports simultaneously. On the one hand, sports have grown in a hostile physical direction in the past fifty years of my life, while new trends of coaching and parenting have emphasized aggressive, but positive competition. Many coaches and parents today are positive with their budding athletes, and do not promote hostile and physically destructive competition. These people don't treat athletes in overly angry and demeaning ways, nor promote hostility toward opponents.

One such trend is led by a sports psychologist from Stanford University, Dr. Jim Thompson.[1] I think the arc of history will move away from today's hostile physical sports world, and ultimately, sports will become caring for everyone involved. Sports will still be aggressive, yes, and have an emphasis on excelling in ability, but be psychologically much healthier. The deep future is going to be better. History will judge us as somewhat primitive in many ways. But humankind will inexorably move ahead in the way we treat one another. And that will be true with sports. Though we are early in its development, the trend is well under way in our time. It will be one giant leap for humankind.

(Dan:) When my father throws me up, it's always just slightly over his head, and it's not so hard and fast. I feel safe the whole time. He's gentle with me. He never scares me with it. And he always gives me a nice gentle hug when he goes to distract me from it. He knows just when to quit. He doesn't keep it going too long until I am into a frenzy for being too wild too long. He knows how to calm me down again. Those other guys don't.

The other types of persons who also show up at what they call family reunions are the ticklers. Once again, I'll laugh just as hard as the next baby when I'm tickled. I admit a little of it is fun. But, again, it's the same guys who toss you too wildly that tickle you too hard and too long.

They seem to get a kick out of seeing kids suffer. This isn't funny business at all. In fact, it's the opposite. Those guys think tickling will make me like them. Frankly, I like the person who just plays with me and follows my lead.

1 Jim Thompson, ELEVATING YOUR GAME, Balance Sports Publishing, LLC, Portola Valley, California, 2011.

Early Parenting for Healthy Development of Athletic Ability: Letting Kids Lead and Roughhousing Gently

(Dan: age 15 months) By now I'm getting big enough to walk, so what I like is someone who is willing to follow me while I choose what playing activity I want to do. Both the warm eyed soft chested one, my mother, and the hard chested one, my father, are really good at this. They give me my lead. As soon as lunch or nap is over, I'll take their hand and they let me lead them to the playroom. They seem to understand people need freedom. I guess some parents fear children being free – they think they will grow up self-centered and rebellious. Grandpa is a psychologist, and he tells my parents the very opposite is true. You'll see how it works as I grow.

When we head for the playroom, I'll just take off in ecstasy. I'll yell on my way, I'm so happy. I love to have them be with me while I explore my play world. They let me choose which toy I want to explore first, and which second. They will enjoy the toy as much as I do. Often they will do the same behaviors I do. If I pick up a ping pong ball and toss it somewhere, they will pick up another one and toss it just like I did.

I laugh big time. I love it. When they enjoy what I'm choosing to do, and do it at about the same skill level as mine, I feel really capable. Their doing what I do makes me happy. Their throwing the ball about just as I do makes me feel good about myself and my throwing ability. I guess not all parents know to do this.

I will lead my parents through rituals of play. I will return to certain toys over and over. I spend up to about five seconds per toy at this age, but my parents don't mind. They just keep moving about from toy to toy, from play experience to play experience. And I love it. And I love them. I love to play with them. People comment how close I appear to be to my parents and how much I like them. They say I'm so secure, healthy and happy. Well, there is a reason. My parents meet me where I am. I'll tell you what I don't like, so if you ever have a little kid just having learned to walk, and you want him to like you, and become confident and strong through his play, you can learn from me. We kids can tell you. We know what we need and what we like. Let us lead you and we'll grow in self-confidence, and our skills will grow along with it. When these relatives come here, I don't warm up to them.

(Grandpa:) Unlike Dan's parents, these relatives cling to the ways of yesteryears. Let me tell you what I mean. They believe that children have to be led and taught. They don't like the idea that they should be following the child while the child chooses what to play with and what to do. They believe they should be "in charge" of the little person. They would be afraid to follow the child in play, for they think the child would grow up selfish and self-centered. The opposite is true. Allowing a child some authority as a toddler, and as a three to five year old, actually will allow the child to get some personal power. That personal power will help the child be a confident and competent person all his or her life. The self-centered and selfish person is a person who was deprived of closeness with a parent.

The self-centered person is a person who never got companionship in these early years, never had parents who followed him into play, who enjoyed what he enjoyed, and who did what the child found pleasurable. He didn't have parents who could enjoy seeing him have authority over his own play. When he was around his parents at this age, his parents tried to teach, direct and control. Let me show you what I mean.

The relatives who come to spend time, the same ones who love tickling and throwing too high, too long and too wild, they are the same ones who won't follow the child into warm companionship play. That's all little kids want. But instead, as soon as theses relatives are in the child's playroom, they spot the basketball hoop and they say, "Dan, shoot the basket." Well, although sometimes Dan shoots baskets - and it's definitely in his ritual of things he loves to do - what they are missing is that right at that moment, he may want to do something else. The basketball shooting isn't where he is right now. Maybe he will want to push cars, or hide under blocks that are piled on him, or simply disorder the play room by going around and pulling things off the shelf and exploring them a minute, then moving on.

If the relative or parent follows the child, and enjoys what the child comes up with, the child would love his or her companionship. But when the parent overlooks where the child is headed and sends a directive for the child to shoot the ball because it's a behavior the parent is interested in, the child will show the parent signs of frustration for sure. This type of parent will interpret this frustrated child as a selfish kid, unwilling to follow adult leadership, and command all the stronger that the child shoots the basketball.

This kind of controlling parenting is done by people who are stuck in the "independent stage" of development themselves and by this kind of behavior they are cultivating children who also will be stuck in "independence". In later chapters I will explain what independent conflicts look like and their destructiveness to marriages, businesses, religions and the world. My book is to explain how the world needs psychological "interdependence" in families, the nation, in the world religions, and between nations. Today too much of the world is stuck in "independence". It causes enormous suffering in the world.

What these uncles and these parents want to see so badly is a child growing in some athletic skill that they love and enjoy. They are focused on getting an athlete in their family, so they can be proud. It's all about them. They are twenty, or thirty, or forty, or sixty, and what they love is sports. They want to develop an athlete. To develop the athlete, they want to see some skill behavior in this little boy. They want him to follow authority, follow a coach.

Well much to their surprise, it's going to be a child who is parented, as Dan is parented, who will be the one following a coach when he's thirteen and sixteen and eighteen, because he will grow up loving companionship with authorities. He will love the rough and tumble of physically age appropriate, safe and gentle wrestling. That will grow as his skill grows in sports or other talents. Dan's parents and grandparents will get to see him living up to his capabilities in sports or other activities. He will be successful because he is getting a foundation of self-confidence, and the love of human companionship.

But the well-meaning, sports loving, uncle or cousin who commands him to shoot the basket is of another world. He is in his world, not the child's world. To play at Dan's level would tax his own attention span not develop Dan's. He would not find it satisfying to follow a little boy or girl into the child's chosen area of play. He would lose out on the great fun and intimacy of following a little boy or girl in play. And the little boy or girl would lose out on the closeness with a male, or female adult, that he or she needs so badly at this and every age.

(Dan:) These relatives continue to try to get the behavior they want to see. "Shoot the basket Dan". I really don't want to do that because I was heading off to something else of my choosing. But they fight for control over me. They insist. They easily pick me up from my path and place me in front of the basketball hoop. They push the ball into my hands and they command, "Shoot the ball".

Never mind that they are asking me to do something at which I will surely fail. I know I can't make it from four feet away. To have success, number one, I need to want to be doing it, and number two, I need some help. If I had chosen the activity and were therefore motivated and were enjoying it, maybe if I'm two feet from the basket, with a gentle and kind lift from the strong arms of the older playmate, maybe the ball would successfully go in and he and I could cheer and clap. I would feel good about myself and be ready to do it again. In this way my skill development would be rightly underway and I would continue to repeat skill building play patterns with this fun loving adult playmate.

The relative who lacks this kind of sensitivity and awareness of children will ask me to do some skill well beyond my capability, raise my anxiety even in the asking, and when I fail to succeed at the activity, convey to me some message of disappointment for my failure. He wants to see me go to the next step of skill, and I'm not there yet, thank you. How about letting me succeed with the skill I do have? Then I'll grow in time. Don't always ask me to do something I can't do. That'll turn me away faster than you can say "Jack Sprat".

(Grandpa:) Now having said all this, I don't want you to think that an adult can never help with skill development. Here's an example of how adults can develop skills in children:

(Dan:) My dad and mom are good at helping me grow in many skills. When we play, they always meet me where I am, and I love it. If we wrestle, they allow me to pin them. I charge them when they are on their knees, and with a mighty push of my hands on their stomachs, they fall over backward, with me on top, by this time, riding them triumphantly to the soft carpet below.

After a bit they will rise up and over I go backward and they gently land me on the carpet on my back and come down on top lovingly hollering, "I pinned you". I am laughing the whole time, and their hollering they pinned me just makes me laugh all the more. What I do is get my little legs up against their stomachs and push them a good one, and again they rise up, this time going over backward with me clinging to their front until they gently land me on the carpet again.

I press my hands against both of their big shoulders and this time I'm the one yelling, "You are pinned". And we laugh with delight. I could do this all day, but they again always seem to know when we have done it enough, and that I need some calming activity instead. This keeps me from being too wild too long and it provides me with soothing that keeps me from getting fussy and overdone with excitement and too much fun. If I went on too long I'd probably get to bawling and mess up the evening of everyone around me.

(Grandpa:) What Dan's parents are doing here is meeting him at his skill level.

(Dan: twenty four months) Actually usually they are performing slightly below my skill level so that I get plenty of chance to feel powerful and competent as a winner. My dad and mom's egos seem to allow them to do this. These big relatives I've told you about, they seem to be threatened by my power, and they play with me in a way that is above my skill level, thinking it will teach me how to do something. But all they've done is make me feel powerless and incapable. I'll shy away from competitive play with them as will their sons and daughters some day, should they have any.

When my dad plays ping-pong with my seven-year-old cousin, or my 15-year-old cousin, he does the same thing. He plays slightly below their skill level because my dad is a darned good ping-pong player. My cousins love to play with him and the score is always close. I see these other big relatives I've been complaining to you about playing in earnest to defeat these cousins and they do. And my cousins I can see with my toddler eyes, don't enjoy it nearly so much. If they lived with these guys, they'd soon quit playing ping pong altogether, because it wouldn't be fun.

(Grandpa:) Traditional parenting didn't know the enormous importance of children's having fun. Fun is fundamental for happiness throughout life. A child learns from her parent how to have fun, kid in an affectionate way, laugh, and enjoy humor. That's a social skill that comes from family. If a parent doesn't model this in early child play, the child may grow without the ability to create fun with people. If the ability to create fun and enjoy friends is stifled in early child development, a person will live a much more bland, boring, and joyless, life, unless it's acquired later from someone else. So, along with skill development in sports or other talents, the ability to have fun is also born in the warp and woof of early child development.

Too often today, one can still hear in our culture people saying: "If you are going to be a good parent, do not try to be a companion or a friend to your child". The exact opposite is true. Or you hear, "The father must be the heavy". Nothing could be further from the truth. In later chapters I'll explain how "interdependence" is the skill both father and mother must learn to do, as opposed to "being the heavy" or "not being a companion to your child." Being really warm and close to your adolescent some day is the very best way to avoid hostile and self-destructive rebelliousness behavior. Believe me we truly have a ways to go before society is healthier for families, couples, and children. All of today's violence and shootings are evidence of how far we must go. The good news is that we do know how to avoid all of this. Already, huge numbers of families experience their kids going through adolescence smoothly, being happy with their parents, and caring about everyone around them. This number will only grow over time. But skill training in schools, churches, and neighborhoods will go a long way towards creating a better, happier, less violent world.

(Dan: 30 months) I guess there are other people in the world like these big relatives. I have a neighbor boy my age named Chucky whose father is like them. His dad is always trying to get Chucky to be a big athlete, even though he, like me, is only 2 ½ years old. He's always trying to make Chucky do something with sports and Chucky shies away from it because it's not fun with his dad. I don't like to be around his father either. As soon as I enter their house Chucky's dad starts trying to make me do something he wants to see me do. It's no fun. I want to do stuff with Chucky that we decide to do.

When Chucky comes to my house, we try to get my dad to play with us all the time if we can. He's fun. What he does is simply become one of us. He does what we like to do. Yes, we end up doing a lot of the same things Chucky's dad wants us to do, but it comes up naturally in our play. Maybe we are having a ball in the basement family room doing whatever, and one of us happens onto a small basketball. Spontaneously we pick it up and run for the hoop. Dad has it set low enough so we can dunk it. It's great fun. At Chucky's house his dad has their hoop set too high for Chucky, and he always demands we try to shoot it up there. Usually we can't make it, and it's not fun. Sometimes Chucky and I will ask my dad to set the hoop higher so we can try above our skill level. If we miss dad just says in an accepting tone, "You missed" and it's OK to miss.

Chucky's dad gets all mad at us when we miss, as if we aren't trying hard enough, and should make it all the time. On those few occasions when we make it, mostly by chance and good luck, Dad and we holler, "hurrah" and jump around in ecstatic celebration, as if it's a great achievement. It's fun. We strive for such moments, but if we miss, it's still fun, and it's OK.

My skills are always improving around my dad, but poor Chucky is all nervous at his house, and he feels he is disappointing his dad all the time. He doesn't want to play over there and his dad gets mad and tries to make him. His dad thinks Chucky is bad and won't try hard to learn more and get better. I don't feel any of that at my house, and it's no surprise that I'm getting a lot better at these athletic things than poor Chucky is. I'll charge the basket like mad, yell when it goes in, and really feel like I'm good at it. Poor Chucky seems nervous all the time, and doesn't seem to play all out, the way I do. I can see why, poor guy. I wish Chucky could live at our house. So does Chucky.

I'll let my dad show me some moves in basketball because he played basketball in middle school and high school, so he knows a lot about it. It's fun to try the stuff he shows me. It only happens when we are already having fun, and it's only when I want to play basketball. If I want to do something else other than basketball, like play with cars or draw and color on the easel, he likes to do that too, because I like to do it. He does that with me too, and it's fun. But when we are playing basket ball, and having fun, he'll show me some moves and I like to try them. He never makes me play basketball nor does he demand I do it out of the blue, like Chuky's dad does.

Chucky's dad is always trying to "teach" Chucky what he, his dad, knows about basketball and Chucky tries to avoid it. His dad gets mad and makes him stand and watch and listen while his dad shows him. Then he makes Chucky do it. It always ends with Chucky's crying and his dad mad at him, telling him he's bad in some way, for the way he is. He says Chucky will never make a good athlete and storms off mad.

Chucky is always nervous around him and really doesn't want to go to basketball games with his dad, but his dad makes him. I love to go with my dad and we yell and carry on. We go home and pretend we are some of the college or pro players. We do the things they do. With my dad it's all fun. I don't feel any pressure from my dad that I have to be a great athlete some day. But I'd like to be if I'm able, because I think it is fun. Chucky feels like he's going to have to be a great athlete or his dad won't think he's any good. My dad says I can be whatever I want to be. It's up to me.

Terrible Twos, Not So Terrible
With Healthy Parenting

(Dan: thirty months) Over at Chucky's house I hear all the time about how terrible the terrible twos are. I don't hear stuff like that at my home. I know I'm 2½ now and quite big, but what's so terrible about me? I know I get upset sometimes. If I'm really enjoying playing something and my folks want us to eat, I can get pretty upset about leaving what I'm enjoying. My parents never get mad at me or say I'm bad for it, like Chucky's parents do. My parents call me to dinner a few times and if I don't come, which I don't if I don't want to, they come and swoop me up lovingly, and carry me off to the table. Sometimes I kick and scream on the way, but usually when I see the food, I start to realize I am hungry and usually I fuss, but let them put me in my big boy chair.

My little brother is in the high chair now, so I'm no longer confined there and if I wish, I can climb down. Usually I don't because I have calmed down by the time we get to the table and the food does look good. I'm starting to feel hungry and I do like being with my family when we eat. It's fun to be with everybody. But occasionally I'm really mad about leaving some really fun play time, so I may keep on yelling when we get to the table. I'll fight going into my big boy chair by splitting my legs out wide so I don't fit. My folks continue to ask me to eat with them, and aren't I hungry and so forth, but they don't get mad at me.

On those occasions and usually I've adjusted by the time I get to the table and calm down and act good, but when I haven't, they usually accept that I'm simply not ready to eat, and they let me run back off to my play, and they continue to eat with my little brother. Eventually I get done with what I'm doing, and I always come back to eat and they keep my food there for me. They aren't mad at me. Usually I'm glad to come to dinner. It's only when I've been especially having fun at play that I don't want to go.

One time I was watching Sesame Street and Mom said, "Dan, I need to go to the store." I protested that I wanted to see the rest of the show. There was ten minutes left. She looked at her watch and said she guessed it would be alright, that she would still have time to get groceries before lunch if we waited. I thanked her.

One other time the same thing happened. She asked me to get my coat and hat and mittens and I said I wanted to watch the rest of the show. She looked at her watch and realized there was 10 minutes left to *Same Street* and said "This time, unfortunately Dan, we can't wait for 10 minutes because we have to be back in an hour to meet Grandma and Grandpa, for lunch". I didn't want to leave and started to yell and cry. Mom after getting little brother set to go, came to me and gently and lovingly but firmly picked me up and put on my coat, hat and mittens, the whole time I'm yelling, and off we went. Halfway to the store I got interested in watching outside the car, and I always enjoy the car, so I stopped sobbing and started to have fun.

At Chucky's house it doesn't go so well. His folks seem to be afraid of Chucky's having any say or asserting himself against what they want. First off, Chucky's mother won't ask him to get his coat on. She orders him to. If he begins to protest, she raises her voice and calls him bad for disagreeing. If he begins to yell or holler, she gets mad. She treats him pretty rough getting his coat on, sometimes pulling his arm hard, or whacking him one on the bottom, the whole time saying he's acting bad and that he's going to be punished more when they get home, like no Sesame Street for three days or something.

(Grandpa:) Chucky's parents are traditionalists. They view things just like their parents and grandparents did without regard for what modern psychology has taught us about parenting. They are very afraid of the strong will of the two year olds. They train Chucky like they used to train horses, and still do sometimes. Namely, that you have to control the child right from the start, in order to establish authority. They are uneasy with the child trying to have some say over himself, and what he does. They believe the parent has to establish control early over the child, so that the parent can control him during his teenage years, so kids won't steal, use drugs or get pregnant early.

They believe kids are born bad, and only with parental control, tight discipline, and a lot of teaching about how to be good, will kids turn out good. Both of Dan's parents grew up without punishment. They were not rigidly controlled and were not told they were bad. Both of their parents were nice to them. They calmly endured when their children were angry or protesting, and they didn't spank or punish in the traditional ways. They didn't use the words "being bad". If you are a parent who has passed on the traditional tapes of your own parents, you might have a hard time with what I just said here. But stick with me, if this is you. This book is to give you new ways to parent. Without new ways spelled out, how could anyone parent differently than they were raised?

Because Dan's parents were raised in a new and different way, they grew up calm and fun to be around most of the time, just as Dan is growing up. They grew up happy, psychologically healthy, and well. It will take time for culture to come around. This book is written to help people know how to parent in a new way. Dan's grandparents already had the human relations skills I will be presenting in later chapters of this book. It was easy therefore for Dan's parents to parent in the same way just as people who don't know the new way, parent as they were parented. Please stay with me and read on.

(Dan: thirty months) My parents know I'll mature out of my strong willed, stubborn and self-centered "terrible twos" as I get older and understand more in a few years. They know I may understand social norms, but do not yet have the controls to do them. They don't fear my strong will and stubbornness.

They see it as an important stage and a sign of a healthy little two year old. My mother doesn't fear waiting 10 minutes until *Sesame Street* is over and setting aside her agenda sometimes so that I can win. And she doesn't fear going ahead and taking me away 10 minutes early sometimes too, when family and other's needs are conflicting with mine, allowing for me to lose.

She knows that the winning and losing to one another is healthier. It's a better pattern to have in family conflicts other than just having the parent win all the time and control all the time. She doesn't fear my having a say sometimes. She knows I will develop empathy for a conflicting party as I grow. She knows that I will learn to give and take, which is essential for a successful adulthood some day. She also believes that if the parents control all the time - thinking they are teaching the child to be a good person - the opposite happens. The child will fight authority, trying to finally get some power.

(Grandpa:) "Strong two year olds sometimes simply go on forever fighting the parent who controls them too much. The stubborn rebellion is established as a pattern that indeed will be there in teenage rebellious behavior, and cause havoc in marriages and businesses. Some kids, strongly controlled, will go another way. Less strong willed kids will learn to adapt so adeptly to controlling parents that they will never have a backbone, never stand up for themselves, never be assertive, or do anything but attach to controlling persons in marriage or at work.

Chucky's dad will control and discipline Chucky right away if ever he sees Chucky try to have his own way. He seems to enjoy it. He thinks his role as the father is to "be the heavy" and make Chucky frustrated whenever Chucky tries to assert his two year old will. He says, "I know Chucky will hate me as a teenager, but that's the role and burden good fathers have to carry." He thinks because he and his dad fought and didn't like each other. because he and his father fought over control, and because he was always trying to do bad stuff in high school to get back at his dad, and his dad was always trying to stop him – Chucky's dad believes that this is the way life is.

Now it is his turn to do the right thing to control tightly, put his son down. He believes he must keep his son in his place, to keep him humble, and control him to be good. He does this because now he looks back and thinks his dad was right and he was wrong. He seems to have little awareness that his parent's original treatment of him, the parent's over-control, resulted in all the anger he had that led to his bad rebellious behavior. He had just bought the messages that he was bad from early off, and believed it. He knew he fought his parents. He was nervous around them and couldn't relax.

He couldn't have fun with them because they were tightly controlling him, thinking they were being good parents. They were doing as their parents had with them, their grandparents with their parents, and on back through the generations. We don't know who started the idea that kids were intrinsically bad, needed punishment, and tight control, etc.

We know the BIBLE said, "spare the rod and spoil the child", so we know that was one place where this belief system got started. There may have been others.

(Dan: age thirty months) When my parents and I conflict and I stand up for what I want, they don't start calling me bad and demand I be good and do what they want "now". Rather they describe their side to me. They tell me why they want me to do something. They give me their reasons. But they also let me know they are hearing what I am saying and that they understand what I want. Just their willingness to listen to my side and let me know they understand how I'm feeling and what I'm wanting helps me hear their side and what they want. I feel more willing to give in after they have talked to me like an adult really. They respect what I want and what I feel.

After this talk sometimes they decide to do it their way, but at least I understand why I have to give up what I want. And they aren't calling me bad because I disagree or want something else. Like most two year olds, I may yell, for not getting what I want when they decide for it to go their way. Or I might yield willingly because of the way they have handled me and respected me. But if I yell they don't get mad or start scolding me like Chucky's father does because they know it's hard for two year olds to give in. They know sometimes I'll yell. They just gently, firmly, and lovingly move me on into what they asked me to do. I soon calm down.

Also, I really don't go ballistic like Chucky does sometimes because I'm not so mad at my parents, like Chucky is. His feelings are hurt and he's really angry with his parents most of the time. My parents say my two year old temper tantrums are usually pretty mild and pass quickly. I'm happy with my parents most of the time. It's only when differences come up between me and them that I have some bad feelings. I quickly get over the bad feelings because I like my parents. They are always good to me. And they say by age five or so, I'll be able to lose to them without going into a big fit of some kind. They understand that maturation in the preschool years is a slow process. They think Chucky will be throwing temper tantrums throughout elementary and even into teenage years or be a defeated door mat, one or the other. His parents always wanted instant improvement and adult like behavior from a preschooler.

My parents never get that look in their eye as if I'm bad like Chucky's parents do. They will tell me they don't like my behavior if I'm difficult, and say what they'd like me to do instead, but they don't spank, hit, scold, or use punishment. They just kind of stand by and stick with me until I get on past something. Sometimes they will physically stop my behavior if they think it's hurtful to me or someone else. But they do it gently, lovingly, but firmly. So I don't feel out of control. And I'm not allowed to violate other's needs, or hurt anyone. I feel well protected.

But I never get the message that I'm a bad person. They know I will behave better as I get some years on me. Because they like me, I can like me. Because they don't see me as bad, I don't have to see myself as bad. If they love me, then I love me. And if they and I love me, then I can easily believe that God loves me. And that's a good feeling.

They also believe I'll live up to my potential. And it's true that I don't hear my parents say stuff like: "You will never be an athlete", or "You will never amount to anything" when they are frustrated like Chucky's parents do. I'm not hearing negative predictions about how my life is going to turn out. My parents think Chucky is getting what they call negative scripting, namely descriptions of how he will fail in some way. They say that carries power in the subconscious. It's no wonder if Chucky doesn't become the athlete he is capable of being.

My parents are comfortable losing to me sometimes when we disagree about what we want to do. They are not afraid to let me have my way sometimes when we differ because they believe that keeps me capable of standing up for myself and describing to others my side of things. They believe that will help me become what they call a "demonstrative" person, someone who can handle conflict, and talk things through with others.

So when they decide to defer to me sometimes, like my mother did by waiting 10 minutes to go for groceries, they know it's good that I got my way instead of bad. At other times they will talk with me, but if their need is pretty strong, they won't mind making me lose to them. They feel that's how I learn to put my needs and wants aside for others. This prepares me to be respectful to authority too, so that when I need to, like at school, I can follow the teacher's leadership.

They believe the kids who are still out-bursting and resisting authority at school are the ones who are in a fight for control at home, as in Chucky's case. Chucky is nervous, hurt and angry. He'll be causing teachers havoc some day. He'll probably need military school as a teenager because he's going to be pretty angry at authority and unwilling to please them if he can help it. Or, if he knuckles under to his parents, which is the other possibility, he'll be meekly passive and dependent. I know his dad won't like that outcome either.

Healthy Ways To Handle The Storminess of The Early Years For Children

(Dan:) I'm so glad my parents seem to handle my upset times with kindness and understanding. I don't know why I'm that way. If I'm doing something I really like, I have a hard time stopping it to do something else. They say I'll grow out of this stage. They say by the time I start school, I'll be well past these outbursts and be able to put aside what I might prefer to do in order to follow the teacher's directions, and I'm sure I will, too, because I'll be a big person then. You have to be pretty big to go to school. I sure look forward to it. I want to ride on the bus. It looks like so much fun.

I've been telling you the bad part of my behavior here and should get back to the good part so you don't think I'm upset all the time. I have a ball most of the time. But before I tell you that part maybe I should tell you the other hard time in my life. I'm so in love with the world and moving around and playing and all that I don't handle being alone in my bedroom for sleep and naps very well. Like I said before I don't like slowing down from my play. I prefer being with people. I love being with other children even though I still tend to play around them rather than with them. I also love being with my parents either with just one of them alone or with the two of them together. I like that.

I can't always fall right to sleep when I'm put in my bed for daytime naps or for nighttime sleep. So as you might expect by now, I'll protest and yell and cry when I know I'm being taken off to bed. I'll try to get extra reading of books. I'll always say "one more", but when they've read one and it's over, I then say "one more" again, hoping to put bed time off as long as possible. Mom just tells me she loves me, kisses me and rubs my back a little when she puts me in and then makes a beeline to the door, even if I'm protesting. Dad will make up another story or two after he puts me in bed and rubs my back awhile. I like the made-up stories. He says he is imparting values through these stories, but I'm too young yet to know what that means.

Someday I'll know and I suppose I'll already have a lot of these values, even though I didn't know what they were. I guess later in my childhood these story times and back rubbing times, will also become a time when I will have my parents' ear if there is anything at all bothering me left over from my day. That chance to express something on my mind will really get me ready to sleep well. And whatever problem I would seem to have would just seem to vanish into the air when I have a chance to tell a caring parent. I really like the tuck-into-bed time even though I don't like their leaving me alone in my room.

What I always do when the door is finally shut and they are gone and I'm alone, is I think about my parents and I feel better. Sometimes I even say to myself, "Mommy Daddy, Mommy Daddy, Mommy Daddy" and you'd be surprised how many times I go to sleep muttering that. Sometimes I'll repeat over and over something they have told me and I picture them telling me it. That makes being alone much easier to handle. Grandpa says kids learn to think by talking to themselves. The sentences they hear from their family become their thoughts. I don't understand that yet, but some day I will. He also says the mommy/daddy repetition is self-soothing.

Let's return to the good things in my life. Since I'm walking now, and have been for quite a while, I love doing it. When I was a baby, I had to sit and manipulate toys and rattles. For a while I put them in my mouth to see what everything felt like to my mouth. I could have eaten the world it seemed. After that, I just felt stuff in my hands. I turned things around and around, seeing how they felt. I would look for buttons in case they would move or light up. I twisted and turned and pressured and slammed them down on the floor. I enjoyed that then and could do it for hours as long as someone would be somewhere in the room. I didn't like to be alone very long.

But now I move around. And do I ever love it. It feels so good to walk and go places. I can go anywhere I want, at least anywhere my parents think is safe. If I start to go toward someplace unsafe, they will box me in rather quickly. I don't always like it, especially if the unsafe place looks interesting, but that's the way it is. I get stopped. I don't always understand and I'll get mad because I don't understand the danger. But at least my parents are kind and they talk to me about what the danger is rather than just stopping me.

My parents say they even talked to me when I was a baby when I didn't understand something and was upset. Even then I guess I could see their sincere and caring faces. That's always helped because now I can see that my parents have a reason for something that I don't understand. They never act like I'm a bad kid or I'm doing bad things when I want to go toward something interesting and dangerous. It's probably frustrating for them to leave what they are doing in order to stop my progress toward getting hurt, but they don't complain or make me feel guilty. They don't get mad at me at those times like a lot of my friends' parents.

If my parents ever do get a frustrating angry tone because something is frustrating for them, they will come back shortly and apologize for the tone. Usually they explain why they were frustrated and got short with me and I can understand. I know they are only human. The apology, however, always feels good because it reminds me that they always love me very much below the surface of life and its frustrations. I'm fortunate because my parents know that at two and a half years old I can't really control what I'm supposed to do. Even though they know I understand already many of the things they want me to do or not to do, yet they understand that I can't always do things, even though I understand them. They say my ability to do the things that culture calls for will come along in time. Some kids' parents think when a little kid can understand something she should be able to do it. When she doesn't do it, she hears from the parent: "You are bad. You're not nice." Labels like this cause bad feelings for kids. I'm so lucky to be free of that.

(Grandpa:) I guess it's easier to say "you are not being nice" than to put into words what the negative effect a child's behavior is having upon you. That takes a little thinking. If parents would do that, the child could know better how her behavior is negatively affecting them. To just say she's "being bad or not nice" is an easy and quick way to express parental anger and frustration. They don't realize what the child records down inside is, "I'm bad. I'm not a good person." And those self definitions lead to failure scripts in life: "I won't make it, or nothing should go right for me", etc.

I saw in my work as a psychologist so many adults who had a hard core of "I'm no good. Nothing will work out for me because basically I'm bad". These feelings and this set of beliefs developed in their early years. It came from parents who knew no other way than to confront frustrating behavior with labels that translated to be "you are a bad kid". I spent thousands of hours of therapy to free adults from these deep-seated feelings that still controlled how these adults felt about themselves. When they worked through the bad emotions inside, and began to see themselves as lovable and good, their addictions and bad behaviors disappeared.

These bad feelings lead people to not believe in themselves. It's the reason for underachievement, whether it is in high school sports or their life work. The sad thing is that the parents who label their kids' difficult behavior as "bad", think they are doing the right thing. They think they are teaching their children what not to do by labeling them as "not nice" or "mean" or "bad boys" and that they will grow up to be nice people.. They have no idea they are giving them an "I'm no good" feeling down inside that results in their not living up to their abilities as teenagers or as adults. These feelings and beliefs also lead to bad behavior and addictions.

It's so much easier to follow all the labels of traditional parenting than it is to think of why the parent doesn't want a certain behavior, and to put into words what the negative effect is, so the child can understand - with his or her thinker - why the parent doesn't want him or her to do it. This new way of confronting frustrating behavior will occur society-wide or nation-wide, or world-wide, only after psychological training for parenting is universal.

Most people can't break out of traditional responses in their parenting because they are ingrained in their minds from their own childhood years. It takes role play and discussion and attempts at interacting in new ways before people can actually do it. When first learning these skills in graduate school, I resisted them as an unnatural way of behaving and talking, but what I was resisting was change. Once into eight-hours-a-day of sessions with people with problems, I learned their effectiveness for making family relationships better. I had the skills before my three kids were born and they grew up so beautifully.

Some people grew up with parents who actually got a kick out of it when a little kid would try to do something that she wasn't quite ready to accomplish, like ride a bike. These parents would laugh at the frustration of the child and this is another way people get bad feelings about themselves. Unfortunately when these kids become adults, they turn around and laugh at their kids in the same way because it's inside them.

(Dan: age three) I'm lucky to have parents who don't do these things. If parents have any of these tendencies because of their childhoods, they should check it when it comes up, so they don't repeat to their children what their parents did. If I have any of this in me, I plan to check it for my kids some day.

Because my parents do treat me so well I certainly do follow all of culture's preferences as much as I can. Some things I can't do yet, but will when I get older and have more control. My parents seem to know the difference. I'm also hearing a lot from people that I am a good little boy. I do sure seem to be a lot calmer and more respectful of others than so many kids my age who seem to be wild, nervous and angry a lot. I'm a fun loving little boy most of the time. People seem to like me. I like that. I will always try to be that way when I get more and more control over my emotions and actions as I grow.

(Grandpa:) Everyone wants a good kid, but so many people yet do not know how to help kids become that way. I am discouraged how so much of the country has returned to tight control, hostile punishments so familiar to traditional parenting. I believe a whole new generation of overly passive and overly rebellious kids will be the result. It may be a generation or two more until modern scientific psychology will be integrated into everyday parenting. Fortunately, a lot of good teachers and a lot of good daycare and preschool workers already have it figured out. They know the difference between the new way and the traditional way, and they won't be going back. Dan has a good daycare and they treat him just like his parents do. The "time out" concept, if used in a firm but caring tone, is a big step ahead of being scolded and punished in the traditional way. However, I advocate talking through frustrations and difficult behavior first however and only using time outs if conflict resolution fails. Sometimes frustrations are too high or time doesn't allow for conflict resolution.

(Dan: age three) Besides playing little cars and driving push toys around, now that I can walk, I love to go outside with one of my parents when he or she has time. I'm fascinated with sticks, fallen trees, birds, rabbits, and berries on bushes. I love bugs, spiders, clouds, the moon and stars. I love to swim. My dad has taken me fishing already and to a baseball game. He gives me tractor rides and trips to the convenience store. Mom takes me to get photos of me and I play at the mall with mobs of kids. I laugh and yell with glee. They took me to a movie too, and it was great.

When I'm tired I'll watch DVDs that my parents say are good for little kids. They read to me when I'm getting tired and fussy. They take me off to bed when I'm sleepy, even if I fight it.

A Tantrum Averted

(Dan: age three) When I reached two and a half years old, I started to get pretty strong about the things I wanted. If I was playing with something I really liked, I didn't like to be stopped for something like a nap or supper. It was hard for me to understand why they would want me to leave such fun for something so much less fun. The nap especially was getting boring.

At least I could see that my parents were kind and understanding when I would get all mad at being taken away from something fun. Chucky's dad and mom would just get mad and start saying he was bad because he didn't want to stop the fun. If Chucky got all mad and cry, they would jerk him around. Sometimes they would even spank him and send him to the bedroom without his meal. I felt sorry for Chucky a lot.

(Grandpa:) Science is in large agreement that frequent spanking (two or three times a week) causes later aggression problems, and cognitive problems for children. Yet, a recent Columbia University study with a representative sample of 1,933 parents found 57% of mothers, and 40% of fathers spank.[2] Parents probably use spanking because they can see the immediate power for stopping unwanted behavior, but they don't realize the long range negative effects for their child. And they don't have skills to handle behavior in a better way. It'll be a giant leap for humankind when parents have a better way than spanking.

---

2 Michael J. MacKenzie (lead author). Study Links Spanking Kids To Aggression, Language Problems. Meredith Bennett-Smith/The Huffington Post. Oct. 22, 2013.

(Dan: age three) One day my dad had picked me up in mom's car where my car seat was. Later we were going to go to the store for some milk and bananas. I loved to go to the store with him, so when he asked if I wanted to go, even though I was playing people and cars, which I love, I was willing to go without being mad. Dad made the mistake of putting me on the back seat of his car where my car seat always sat. He told me that he'd be right back with my car seat, since he had to get it from Mom's car. I realized while he was gone that it felt really good just sitting like an adult there in the spot my little kid seat usually sat. When Dad arrived with my car seat, I told him to take it back, that I'd just sit on the big seat like bigger people do.

He said no, I had to let him put me in my chair. I started to get louder because it seemed unfair to me. I couldn't see why it wouldn't be OK for me to sit like the bigger people do. I didn't want my little kid seat. Later I learned that Dad was trying out some different approaches that Grandpa had told him about that came from psychology.

First he tried out what was called tough love. That was what they liked to do with the kids who turned to taking drugs, not studying at school and stealing from department stores. He tried getting tough and saying, "If you don't get in the seat, we can't go to the store. That's just the way it is." (I guess they call this "threatening" & "negative reinforcement" that is, taking away privileges.) I was pretty good at talking by now, so I said, "Yes, we can go to the store". "I'm big enough to sit here and you know how to drive. We can go to the store."

Dad didn't get mad or start telling me I was bad. He decided to try the next theory. He reached in his pocket and pulled out a handful of coins, and said, "If you get in the car seat, you can have this". (I guess this is called "positive reinforcement", which is offering a reward.) Since his hand held out the change and since I really liked playing with money and saving it in my piggy bank for Sunday school, I reached out and took the money. He smiled and so did I. I like money. He said, "Will you move over so I can put your car seat in now?" I just smiled and shook my head "no". I also kept the change.

So finally Dad decided to take the time to try a third theory of child rearing. He sat next to me and told me about a legislature that made rules and laws. I didn't understand those words and I could tell he knew that. But at least he was talking nicely to me and didn't get mad and start saying I was being a bad kid. Instead, he went on to think about how I did understand policemen and firemen. He said the police didn't let us do things that might hurt us. I knew about getting hurt and being careful, so I understood that idea.

He said if we drove with me sitting like a big person that the police could stop us and Dad would have to pay lots and lots of money. He said it was to keep children safe. He said the police believe kids are safe in these car seats. He showed me if there was a crash, although he promised to drive safely and carefully, that the back of the front seat would protect me so I wouldn't get hurt. He said, the child's seat would also keep me safe in a crash. I knew what crashes were because I played crashing with my play cars. I knew that when I fall down and crash I get hurt. So I could see what my Dad was explaining. I understood. He could see I understood. He said, "Now will you get in the car seat?" I agreed to and got over so he could put in the seat and I climbed in.

(Grandpa:) Chucky's parents never talked nicely at show down times like this. They have swung back to tradition, like much of our culture has. They believe kids grow up self-centered and rebellious if you don't keep a heavy hand on them. They believe that tight control over kids early in life results in a nice personality that obeys rules and authority for a lifetime.

They think permissive parenting results in rude, rebellious and self-centered kids. It'll take another generation before they find out tight control, when people are little, isn't going to do it. You'll get yes men or rebels, and there is a better way. But most parents lack the skills to confront and handle the two year old in the right way. If Dan, the three-year-old, could use big words, he would put it this way:

(Dan: age three) I think my parents are doing it right. I sure do like them. And for example, you can see how my Dad handled the car seat showdown. Two-year-olds can be respected in spite of their stubbornness and they can reason and learn democratic decision making even in conflict. The third way of parenting that my dad tried asks parents to take a deep breath when conflicts come up, and do some relationship conflict resolution skills.

(Grandpa:) First you tell the child what you want to do, in this case get the car seat and go to the store. If the child complies, there's no problem. If the child digs in to resist, then instead of using threat, telling him he is bad in some way, like he's naughty or a bad boy or whatever, the parent starts a back and forth communication skill. The parent, seeing the resistance, does what's called active listening, namely, summarizes what the child is wanting. In this case the parent says, "So you like sitting like a big person and don't want to get in the child seat?"

So already the child feels like a person whose wants and feelings are important to the parent. Instead of being called bad for wanting a say in this situation, he is respected. The parent's tone of voice is always accepting when he summarizes what he perceives the child to be feeling. If the parent conveys frustration and ridicule in his voice while summarizing the child's view point, that shows the parent can't get out of his own desire for the child's immediate compliance. And the child, of course, remains in a power struggle mode for which three year olds are universally known.

But with skill training, which very few parents ever get, a parent can learn to demonstrate this kind of empathy in conflict with her toddler. Hopefully the parent has the ability to have empathy in conflict with his spouse as well, because power struggles are just as commonly destructive to adult love relationships as they are between toddlers and parents. The skill of expressing your own preference (namely to get in the car seat) but then switching to "hearing" the child's side of the issue through active listening or summarizing the child's view, is a very mature thing to do. Most people blunder on with the power struggle in such moments, label the child as bad for being a typical healthy two year old, and force the issue either by threats, giving or taking away privileges. They finally just force the child to comply.

This, of course, results in the temper tantrum. Admittedly, sometimes parents don't have time to use good communication skills at such frustrating times, and because of the clock, they may start by asking, then listening, but have to give in to forcing since there isn't time to do the talking that I demonstrated here. But at least if the parent knows the skills and can use them most of the time when not under time pressures, the chances for the child to grow in a healthy conflict resolution way are still good. Parental forcing resulting in the temper tantrum sometimes is inevitable and won't hurt the child, especially when the listening, understanding and caring tone of voice accompanies the need to force and move on. When the "you are a bad kid" messages are simply left out of such conflict times, the child is not going to carry a very big load of "I'm bad" feelings inside. No load of "I'm bad" means a person grows with a sense of trust in his or her own developing capabilities. As adults, people can live up to their potential instead of falling short.

Too often parenting is seen as either too authoritarian or too permissive. Generally parents kind of struggle with these two options, feeling guilty if they go either way. You can see from my example of a parent skilled in the use of psychological skill training that there is a third alternative to these two. Those in the past fifty years who have run back to authoritarian parenting of small children - out of their fear of drugs, early teen promiscuity, and teenage rebellion - haven't gotten the privilege of psychological skill training as an alternative to authoritarianism or permissiveness. Both authoritarianism and permissiveness in my judgment result in passive kids, rebellious kids, or self-centered kids. Recently, I viewed Katie Couric's show that featured the issue of parenting today. Everyone who spoke reflected the confusion of today's parents. Everyone was aware that over control isn't good – the current term is "helicopter" parenting – but everyone in the discussion at some point did a one eighty, and added: "But make sure you control your kids". This is about where most American parents stand today, stuck between these two concepts. It's a miserable position within which to operate as parents.

When children are raised with skilled parents, there are no passivity problems, rebellion problems or self-centered problems. Kids grow up assertive, able to communicate when in conflict, able to yield when necessary, and competent. They live within society moral standards and don't get into self or other destructive behavior. They don't have to hate their father as the heavy. They remain friends with their parents throughout all the stages of their lives.

I demonstrated in the child seat example how a child can yield after good communication. This was an issue where it was necessary for the parent's way to prevail. My model of communication holds that 80% of differences can be resolved peacefully with a consensus or compromise. In this example they both agreed after talking, and the temper tantrum from win-lose dynamics, didn't have to occur. The other 20% is when no consensus or compromise can be reached and one or the other needs to simply give in. When a parent learns to actually use listening skills (which most untrained parents won't) in 10 % of conflicts, the parent actually understands the youngster's view point enough, and realizes his own preference doesn't have to prevail. He can gracefully yield to the child.

Hearing the child's side so often alleviates parental anxiety and the parent can see it's OK for the child's preference to take place. The parent demonstrates "losing", or "letting go", capability. The parent, by letting go of his side, is modeling for the child to learn to let go gracefully. Each side needs to let go, according to my model, 10% of the time. Letting go is only necessary if consensus can't be reached.

What is good for the child when she gets her way is the ability to be competent, help define her own destiny, stand up for herself, etc, all the things that keep her on tract to be an adult who can express feelings, conflict respectfully, and have a say over her own life. This makes a good executive, a good employ, a good adult love partner. Conversely, when a child gets the ability to gracefully lose after communication in conflict, and the parent's way prevails, a child has an invaluable tool for getting along with authorities and other people.

A person raised by authoritarian parents is susceptible to loss of trust when in conflict. This person may quickly escalate anger and can only defend his or her own side hoping to win. He never had anyone listen to his side in conflict, so he doesn't have the ability to listen to others. He only knows the power struggle, to win or lose without communication or agreement to do so. He doesn't know what working things out feels like. Likewise, a person raised with permissive parents would have a sense of entitlement, thinking he could dominate and win in all situations. Nobody likes such persons, whether raised by authoritarian parents or permissive, unless such persons grow into communication skill capability. They don't make good executives. They don't make good parents. They don't make good employees. And they don't make good marital partners. No wonder the divorce statistics are so high.

I had a boss for twenty years who could communicate when we had a difference. Usually we could nicely find a consensus. When it wasn't possible after talking, one or the other of us would agree to yield to the other. Sometimes he let me do my preference; sometimes I yielded to his. With a boss, of course, the boss gets to decide when he yields or when I will yield, because his role is defined by society to be ultimately responsible for what goes in the work place. This, of course, is also true for the parent who has legal responsibility for a child. It's the parent who decides when she will lose or when she will win.

In an adult love relationship, of course, this is not true. I believe marriage partners are equal, so one or the other partner decides to yield if consensus cannot be met through the back and forth communication skills. The important thing in an adult love relationship is that it does go back and forth, where each yields from time to time. Otherwise, if it always goes one way, then you are back into dominance and submission. Dominance and submission aren't healthy and can result in loss of love, especially for the losing partner. Although there are exceptions, in my experience of thirty six years as a marital therapist, it's the losing partner who mostly reaches out to affairs in an attempt to regain love that no longer exists in her marriage. It's the dominant partner who so often is surprised and baffled by his partner's loss of love. We human beings have to have a say over our lives to retain our love for our partners.

It's popular now for many parenting programs to condemn any kind of talking or listening when in conflict with children, as if any talking is nothing but attempts on the children's part to manipulate away from compliance. Unfortunately this view is being seen through the eyes of those who have run back to strong parental control as the only answer for parents. And it's not surprising that they view talk as manipulative, because once parents are into strong control, the result is children who are in a power struggle. Children in power struggles, like adults in power struggles, do begin to manipulate, to try to have some say over their lives. Over-controlling parents will be surprised that they end up with a manipulative child. Sadly, I've seen children who are sneaky, conniving manipulators of the first order. They lie, cheat, and do anything to attempt to get their way. Unless turned around, their lives will become a museum of lost opportunities. They will not succeed in all the ways that make people truly happy.

Healthy Handling of Elementary-Age Sibling Conflicts: The Parent Is A Traffic Cop

(Dan: age seven and a half) I'm bigger now and my parents say I'm a world easier to deal with. I can get myself up, dress myself, and do most everything for myself. In our family one of the things we do is that I get to go out individually with each of my parents for breakfast once a month. They say they see my best adult personality coming on in these one-to-one breakfasts. We talk about ideas for vacation. We talk about what I'm into at school. They tell me about their jobs. We make plans for fun things to do as a family during these times and I feel really special. I look forward to these times. Dad and I do fishing trips together. We go to ball games together. He has taught me to fish. Mom takes me shopping for clothes that I need. Sometimes Dad takes me shopping too. Mom takes me to special kid's days. Those are fun and special days to me.

You are probably wondering how my difficult behavior is coming by now. I mentioned to you before that my parents believed that I would be able to let temper tantrums go by the time I went to school. They said I would be able to pay attention at school and when asked, I could stop doing fun things in order to get back to work. Actually, I'm proud to announce I can do all those things. I'm considered by my teacher to be one of the enjoyable and cooperative boys in my class. The temper tantrums are long gone for me, whereas some kids in my class are still into them. I can play with peers and I do a good job athletically. This helps a lot with being a part of the recess games.

One of the rough spots at home now is when my brother and I fight. I am seven and a half. He is five and a half. We mostly enjoy one another and are the best of buddies most of the time. If I get home first thing in the door, I say, "Where is Brad"? When he gets home the first thing in the door he says, "Where is Dan"? We are playmates and enjoy most of the same activities. We have the basement set up for roller skate hockey since we are both goalies on the hockey team during the winter months. We can play roller hockey by the hours in the summer. We also play basketball outside. When the neighbor kids come, we play baseball on our lawn. We have a tree house and can play outside for hours with neighbors in the spring and summer and fall.

We have competitive sports through park and recreation and take piano lessons. We do recitals occasionally and play baseball, soccer, basketball, and tag football, depending on the season. I love life and am a busy boy, as you can see. Our parents haven't pushed us into any of this. We just got busy with some of these skills early because our Dad or Mom played them with us after daycare and on the weekends. Not all kids are into athletics like we are, and that's OK. They find their own activities to enjoy and do. Often it depends on what their parents saw were their interests and abilities, and got them started early too.

Now back to the rough spots that I mentioned above. My brother and I can get into squabbles. Most of the time we're fine and like each other. Here's what our parents do. Typically we will get frustrated over something we both want at the same time. Usually these times happen just before dinner, when everyone is tired and hungry. Sometimes it happens when we need to do something that's not so fun, or we've had an overnight with friends and we're worn out for lack of sleep.

Ever since we were little, if we fought, our parents might stay out of it if it were some little scrap. But if it gets bigger than that and people are angry, maybe hollering at each other or someone crying, our folks will come. If we have begun to tussle, they firmly but gently pull us apart physically. One thing our parents say we don't ever do is hit in the face or hit hard like some kids do. If we get physical, it's usually wrestling or if we hit, it is controlled hitting that isn't aimed to hurt badly. Mostly it is aimed to hurt feelings instead. Our parents say the reason we don't go all out with the violence to hurt badly is that we've always been treated well. Therefore, we don't have it in us to hurt badly. I think they are right.

What happens when they part us and sit down between us? They ask what's going on between us. When one of us begins to complain about the other usually the other tries to cut him off. One will start up talking in order to blame the other, and get his own side represented. The first thing our folks do is get us stopped long enough to establish that one is going to go first and the other will talk next.

They enforce this, if either of us tries to break back in before our turn, they remind us to wait and give our undivided attention back to the first speaker. My parents never judge what is being said. They know it is one person's perspective and the other will have his turn. They work to understand the speaker to make sure the speaker's side gets out in its entirety. They may even repeat or paraphrase what the speaker is saying. This way everyone is crystal clear how the first party feels about this altercation. They know we may over exaggerate a bit when we're hurt and angry, but they don't scold us for that either. They just listen.

The parent turns to the second person after the first person gets his viewpoint out. If I'm the second to speak, now it's my turn to complain and rant and rave about how I'm angry, hurt and have been mistreated by my brother. I will say what he did wrong from my viewpoint and make a case for why I was justified for getting upset and so on. If my brother tries to cut back in my parent will stop him so I get my say in full.

When each side has gotten out his hurt and anger, my parent leads the way in asking if anyone has any solutions for how this problem could be solved. We have gotten out all our hurt feelings and are now feeling listened to, cared about, and heard. Because the hurt feelings are expressed and gone and we feel better, we are in a better place to come up with some solution that we can live with. Now we are ready to return to play. Usually the solution is to share some toy by each getting it for five minute intervals until someone is ready to move on to another toy. This is a common solution.

Since our hurts and angers have been expressed and gotten rid of, we can now agree on something constructive. Our parents always asks for our potential solutions first, and sometimes they will throw one or two in also. They always ask us first. It's amazing how we now feel ready to cooperate . When this is all done, our parents will return to getting dinner or whatever they were doing. Our parents feel the time spent in resolving fights this way is a positive investment in our futures.

My parents say that they understand that kids fight sometimes and they say most all relationships have their conflict times. They don't label us as bad for our occasional fighting. They know it's normal for our age and recognize it happens in all relationships, including their own. They say they are giving us skills to handle conflict in future marriages or jobs.

(Grandpa:) A lot of parents get mad with their kids fighting, and come at their kids with labels of badness. This is designed to make the kids feel guilty for their fighting, as if that would lead them to be better and therefore be non-fighting kids. What happens is parents give vent to their own frustrations. Maybe they had a bad day or are hungry and tired too, so they lash out with anger in the same immature way their kids do. Most parents shame the older of the two fighting children, so that child gets the biggest amount of "I'm bad" feelings out of sibling fighting, to carry deep within for the rest of his life. Some parents believe in hitting, thereby demonstrating, I guess, that hitting is the way to go when you are mad and fighting.

Other parents will approach the kids with a whole lot of anger, ordering kids to stop it. Some will immediately mete out punishment like, "Go to your room", or announce withdrawal of privileges, or say they will ground their kids from highly likable activities like movies or times with friends, or something they really love. Some just announce the more civilized "time out", but I think with "time outs" parents are teaching kids to simply withdraw from conflict instead of learning communication skills to work on through the conflict. However when there isn't time to talk, or when emotions are way too strong, the "time out" may be the best alternative.

If I ever came off in these negative ways when my kids were fighting, I would come back very soon and apologize. If parents have had a bad day or they are feeling tired or down for some reason, they may come at their kids in this way because the old traditional tapes are rolling in their heads. It's the way parents used to behave before parents understood the research findings of modern scientific psychology.

Kids can see it when a parent is over frustrated and being irrational in monitoring their fighting, but it sure feels better to the kids when their parent apologizes at such times. It also serves to teach the kids that parents are only human and they can overreact sometimes out of frustration. Apologizing erases any bad feelings kids may have gotten from their parent's overreaction and allows the bad feelings and messages to fade. It doesn't leave emotional scars or bad self concept messages stuck down inside to cause trouble in the future. Any of the usual emotional scars and bad self feelings can dissipate instead of remaining inside the child, only to grow bigger with each new conflict.

When parents get frustrated or angry with one another over some issue, they, too, can sit down and work on it. They, of course, won't have a referee like children do. They will sit down and face the difference. They will allow themselves the same first stage of a conflict, which is venting exactly what they are angry and hurt about. Each agrees to the structure to let one go first and complete what that one needs to say before the other interferes or starts to talk.

After each gets a chance to let the other hear how he is hurt or angry, and why it is he feels that way, it is much easier to handle the conflict. During each one's turn, he can say what he thinks the other is doing that leads to the hurt and anger. When each has done this, a considerable more understanding has taken place about each partner's side. Again the anger has been released. The hurt has been released, maybe one or both will cry in the process, just like kids sometimes do. Then a third stage begins where they, too, search for solutions to their conflict.

It's easier to return to thinking rationally after hurt and anger has been honestly expressed. When expressed and listened to, these feelings evaporate and each person is more ready to look for answers, solutions and new ways for handling this issue. When bad feelings happen between partners, it means something has been brewing and there is some difference that needs to be brought out in the open and examined.

The way parents deal with sibling conflicts will set the stage for how their children handle conflict in their marriages later in life. You can see this way of dealing with sibling conflict makes more sense than confronting kids, saying that they are bad, sending them to their rooms, or simply punishing them by a withdrawal of privileges. What guidance would any of that give kids for adult life other than give them more of the "I'm no good" baggage to carry? They would be left without communication capabilities to solve relationship conflicts.

For a lot of parents it's just so easy to give in to their own frustrations and it's gratifying when they are frustrated to be angry at their kids. It's so easy to lash out with punishment and scolding. This feels a lot better to the parents when they are frustrated, than it does to be mature, calm and sit down and listen to the difficult emotions of their children's hurts and angers. But it doesn't feel better later when the parents feel guilty and they know deep within it couldn't have been the best way, to handle it. This is especially so since they know their kids, whom they love deeply, are in their room hurting and feeling bad about themselves.

When parents referee their kids and let them express their viewpoints and their hurts and angers, lots of feedback takes place. Each has to listen to the other person's story. Each gets a lot of truth about his particular contribution to the misunderstanding. When dealing with sibling conflict in this way, each can see how he contributed to the development of bad feelings. Each can hear his opponent's pain. This causes each one to care about the other and think how each could avoid hurting the other another time.

If you never stopped to hear the hurts and angers or let the partner talk, you would never have learned from it. If conflict areas are left to simmer unresolved, more and more aspects of a relationship become affected. Love feelings might be lost if repair doesn't take place.

That's exactly why a lot of people lose love in marriages. Eventually divorce is the only option if love has died. This is a tragedy. Young Dan has a good shot at adult love success and satisfaction because of the way his parents understand dealing with child sibling conflicts. I don't think Chucky has a prayer.

Parents want their kids to be equipped to constructively handle conflict in their future love relationships. They want them to have the skills to help their kids resolve and solve conflict so that their kids can take care of their adult love relationships some day. If recurring anger is left inside to boil, it only leads to further fighting. Then you get a downward cycle that isn't good in family life.

Chucky's parents knew nothing of getting emotions out during times of conflict. They only knew how their parents handled sibling conflicts. Namely, conflicts were to be approached as if someone was misbehaving. Someone needed to be punished. Quarreling children were to be scolded and someone was to be blamed for the conflict, one or both. This traditional approach was based on a belief that if you were a good child causing no trouble you'd be a good adult some day.

The Healthy Parent Is A Referee

(Dan: age Nine) Now besides the sitting down with us to express our sides of a fight, my folks do another thing in our family to deal with conflicts. They call this the "family conference". They say there are times when everyone in the family seems to be getting on one another's nerves. This is when apparently a number of conflicts are going on that cause frustration and conflict in our daily lives. They can tell it's happening when there seems to be more fighting than what is customary. There is more frustration and more moments of feeling bad.

What happens is that someone sees it and announces that it's time for a "family conference". We always moan and groan when that idea comes up because it seems like there is a fear of it before we do it. I guess it's the honesty it's going to require when people sit down to admit their bad feelings about things. So we all kind of resist it and it doesn't always happen right on the original time we set. But it always happens eventually after it's been announced and planned.

This time everyone in the family sits down together and one of the parents is the referee again. By referee we mean a person is the one who makes sure each person gets her turn to talk without being interrupted or put down. We always start those meetings with high anxiety, it seems. Usually the referee parent begins with how stressful and conflicted family life has been around here lately and that this meeting is for the purpose of dealing with it. The rules are always mentioned, namely that everyone is going to get his turn to talk about the issues from his viewpoint.

As soon as one person is given the floor, we invariably start to bombard one another. It is so natural to vie for attention. People try to immediately shoot down whatever is beginning to be said. It always feels like the whole thing is going to explode. Everyone feels pretty uncomfortable in the beginning. It always seems to take a while, maybe five minutes or so, before this first uncomfortable stage begins to pass. I suppose for a lot of families, it could break down here and people run away from it, each to their own next task or event. But our family has had so much success with this that we know it works. It clears away stress and conflicts so that everyone gets more loving and fun when the meetings are over. Then we get on with our lives in the days to follow, much the better off as loved ones living in the same space, a home.

(Grandpa:) After the high anxiety stage finally passes, and the first person gets into what he is feeling, what his complaints are, and how he thinks he is being short changed in some way, and by whom, gradually the success of the therapeutic gathering begins to be felt. Sometimes a person may be tearful when he describes how he is feeling. Everyone becomes empathetic. That person feels it too. It begins to feel very good, even though it hurts. It begins to feel very right, needed and very necessary. Now your loved ones understand how you have been hurting.

One by one, family members take their turn in speaking to what's been going on. What are they hurting about? What are their needs that have been going unnoticed or neglected? Who do they think has mistreated them in what way? Actually it's an airing of how a person feels deep down inside. Something very magical and powerful happens when a person speaks honestly about his pain or wants and needs. People feel for him. People for the first time realize what this individual is going through. Now they know what he needs from others, in the family. It feels so good to get it expressed to others even though at the time it may hurt emotionally. By now he is feeling that it is a safe environment. No one is anxious now. No one would put him down. Everyone is in a listening and caring stage.

One by one, each family member gets to tell his own story. When everyone has spoken, now the leader, the refereeing parent - sometimes both parents play this role at the same time - will say: "OK, what ideas do people have for what we need to do?" Problems are identified and solutions roll. Even if every complaint doesn't get time for brainstorming solutions, it's amazing how much improved the climate is in the home in the days to follow.

The anxiety is down. The affection and fun are back up and primary. Now family members feel cared about, understood and supported. They know they are in a loving family. Everyone feels loved again, as it should be.

The key for this family conference is that the referees must stay neutral. Their role is to keep people in early stages from butting in and starting up attack and counterattack when anxiety is still high. If parents slip back into judging, criticizing, or trying to tell people what they should or should not be doing, which is viewed as normal traditional parenting, this family conference will not work. Such interventions will only set up the usual push-pull that is so typical of most parent child problems. Sooner or later society will get around to skill training so the referee parent learns to hold back his own first immediate reactions, his view, his advice, and his wants. Instead, he needs to be the person who makes sure everyone feels safe to talk openly. This is a known psychological skill.[3] It is the application of the active listening (repeating) skill described above. It may be a generation or two before this skill gets out to the average person in society. It's a luxury that society doesn't recognize. Society has too many other problems demanding time, money and attention. When society can get around to doing parent skill training, it will result in one giant leap for humankind. Or will FY2017 start it?

The refereeing parent only protects the speaker, clarifies what he or she is saying for understanding, and raises the offer for all to brainstorm solutions after everyone has safely talked

---

3 Rogers, Carl R. Client Centered Therapy: Its Current Practice, Implications, and Theory. Boston: Houghton Mifflin, 1951.

about his or her view of family stresses and conflicts. Of course, the referee parent gets his turn to talk too. Usually he will go last, however. Kids that grow up in families that handle conflict in this way like their parents. They can talk with their parents when they need help and support in their lives. They don't have to become enemies during their teenage years and they don't have to become rebellious rule breakers or passive and dependent. I don't like hearing people say that good parenting means the parent has to be the heavy or that kids will naturally not like their parent if their parent is being a good parent.

I don't like the assumption that "kids will be kids", meaning they have to do self-destructive rebellious things during their teenage years. I especially grieve the pattern where people grow up fighting with their over-controlling parents and then turn the coin to become over-controlling parents themselves. Once they have children of their own, they look back to their control battle with their parents. They conclude their parents were right to be controlling and that they were the culprits, the bad rebellious kids. So, unfortunately, they switch over to their parents' philosophies and start over-controlling their kids and the battles start all over for the next generation. In twenty years of consulting to a youth drug treatment program and a children's residential treatment program, I saw this pattern over and over again.

I have been describing the family conference in Dan's home. Now let's look at what's happened in Chucky's family at the same stressful time of year. It is mid-terms or finals at school. Chucky's brother has gotten into a fist fight twice in the last week. Chucky is not functioning at school academically. Chucky's sister is dating an abusive guy. Chucky's parents are at their wits end. They try to lecture the boys about fighting. They withdraw privileges. They ground them. They tell their daughter to not see this guy ever again. And the kids just tune them out. The kids feel criticized and controlled. No warmth or connection or understanding takes place.

All three kids try to stay away from home as much as possible. Even though they've grown up in a church, it is hard for any of the kids in this family to feel there's a loving God in this universe. Only clouds ride over their heads. They turn to addictions for solace. Even by middle school age, the boys take antisocial routes. Their sister seeks to marry a destructive boyfriend and get out of the house early. Everyone seems to be hurting everyone else and the traditionally defined forgiving God has to wait patiently until anyone might turn to some faith that emphasizes forgiveness of sins and getting a clean slate to start over. Some will turn to such faiths at some point along the way, usually after years of addictions and anti-social activities.

Maybe the daughter will seek such a faith after release from a women's shelter that helps protect her from more spousal abuse. Maybe the boys will turn to such a faith after years of drug and alcohol involvement that has its inevitable outcome in wild party physical fights, stealing for money, and lost relationships. A church that emphasizes God's forgiveness with the right to be washed white as snow may be the church they will need.

Getting attention for telling their stories of depraved behavior in the past, and being received with respect and open arms may just become the new world they need to get started over. With the help of the church, if they rigidly avoid all their tendencies of their past, they may begin to get some new stability. If they feel surrounded by the love of people they will see each Sunday and perhaps in a few small group meetings per week, they may feel something they never felt growing up, and their behavior will change. Will they learn to talk honestly, listen carefully to others or another: will they learn to conflict resolve rather than control and be controlled: I hope so. It would help if such skill training were available in their church.

If children grow up in families like Dan's, they don't have to take the routes of addictions, anti social behavior and choose abusive relationships. These are all behaviors the traditional church would have seen simply as man's depraved sinful state. Without psychological skills prior to the last century it is no wonder church leaders took to the idea of man as sinful who was forever in need of salvation from unavoidable sin. In Dan and his wife's family, no child grows up being harmful to others. Children who are loved with parents who have democratic conflict resolution skill capability have no evil intentions. The only trouble that occurs in relationships is when people want different things, and with skills they can move through those conflicts without controlling, abusing or harming one another.

The church of the faithful then can become for healthy individuals a place of worship and positive fellowship. They don't need to spend time hearing of the sinful testimonials and how God has brought new birth, so that for the first time in their lives they could get free of destructive behaviors. For healthy people growing up in healthy relationships, the idea of sin and salvation from sin is no longer needed. These people aren't born in sin. They haven't grown up being sinned against, and they will not go out into the world sinning against other people. Their church life will be positive worship of God, positive companionship with other church members, and their focus will be on helping society become more loving to all people everywhere.

Universal skill training could result in a growth in churches, temples and synagogues that worship in this way. The traditional church, temple and synagogue that struggle to mend the abused, destructive and dangerous person could be free to become a healthier type of fellowship and worship. A world that no longer produced damaged and dangerous people, and produced healthier forms of worship, would be a giant leap for humankind. After all, don't most religions, at core, call for a universal loving brotherhood and sisterhood of humankind? Wouldn't a loving God, trying to come through the religions of the world, want healthier and happier families?

The Healthy Parent Is A Taxi Cab Therapist

(Dan: age ten) I think our happy home is the base, so to speak. Since I feel good inside, I can put a lot of energy into the pursuits I love. One of the things you will find when you are a kid in lots of sports is that you get plenty of practice in losing. My parents are not just taxi service personnel. They are there to pick up the pieces when some important games go south. Nothing feels much worse than to lose in some huge game by, say, one point. This is especially true if you were the one that missed the free throw that would have thrown your team into overtime. Had you made the basket, you would have been the great hero. You would have been the one who lifted your team's spirits and led them into overtime. Your team would be so pumped over your basket that they would most likely go on to win. They would win because they now have the confidence and the momentum. You would be the great hero for a day or so.

Riding home after a horrible let down in sports can be a pretty glum experience. I can hardly wait sometimes to leave my sad buddies and get in the car. Once in the car, I know my parent will be talking to me about all that I did so well in the game and how next time the shot would probably go in since I have a really good shot. I've cried more than once on the way home from difficult games and felt a heck of a lot better by the time I got home to dinner.

One time I rode home with Chucky and his dad when Chucky had made a lot of mistakes in the game. Chucky said almost nothing. His dad did all the talking. He was telling Chucky all that he "should" have done. He told him all the moves Chucky should have done rather than the ones he did. His dad believes he is teaching Chucky something by all this talk about what he did wrong. But I believe he is simply driving Chucky further and further away from him. I can tell you I asked my parents not to have me ride home with Chucky's dad again. I just couldn't stand what he was doing to Chucky. That day I sent up a little prayer of thanks for my parents when I got out of that car.

My parents talk about what I did right and they reassure me about any mistakes I made. My parents mostly listen and I am the one talking. They listen quietly most of the time. I'm so excited I want to talk to them about the game. They point out things that happened in the game that were really quite good. I leave those talks feeling boosted in confidence and good about myself.

As I say, my parents are really a life saver when I leave difficult games. The same is true, however, when I leave really great games where my friends and I prevailed in throwing over some great opponent. Actually, even every day games that aren't such big games also result in rides home that are fun. Most the time after games I'm talking a mile a minute. My parents are mostly listening, but they are excited too. So between me and them there is a lot of fun remembering moments in the game. Some moments were funny.

Some are times I'll always want to recall so I'm talking, according to Grandpa, to seat them well in my memory banks. If my feelings were hurt in any way by what someone did or said, usually those kinds of feelings, though not so big, are expressed and thereby forgotten so as to not affect my relationships next time. To get it off your chest is a great thing. It kind of keeps you clean with people on the inside, so to speak. If someone yelled something in the heat of the moment that wasn't so complementary, if I tell it to my parents after the game, it's forgotten and forgiven. All they have to do is listen. Grandpa says parents too often think they have to talk and teach. He says the truth is the healing takes place by the child talking and the parent just being there. What I've described here for athletic events is true for all the other non-athletic activities that kids participate in: music, theater, art, hobbies, and kid's organizations of all kinds. The parent's caring involvement is critical to success and confidence in all areas.

This is one way that I'm really connected to my parents. They are there, at those times to be excited with me or to hear my frustrations and hurts. If for some reason they can't be there then there is always the tucking in bedtime when they are there to hear about my day, good and bad.

At church they say God made the world because he wanted companionship. They say he gets a kick out of the great and good games too and hurts with us after a loss. I can really believe in a God like this because my parents are that way. I wonder if it's hard for Chucky to be a believer in any loving personal God. I can see why he might throw it all out as wishful thinking. I hope Chucky someday gets someone who could care for him in a loving way like my parents. Then he could begin to believe there might actually be a good God who does care.

I ask my parents: How could there be a transcendent loving God who could actually know what's going on in the lives of eight billion people here on earth? They say anyone big enough to cause an explosion that shot one hundred billion suns out into our solar system would be big enough to hear eight billion prayers at once. We are talking huge here, aren't we! I guess if he has a big brain, it's not limited to paying attention to one or two little things at a time like ours is.

The Healthy Parent Is A Bedtime Therapist

(Dan: age eleven) At age eleven I still get a back rub each night and Dad still tells me stories that he makes up. I love to hear what he will come up with each evening. It's a time that I can tell him about my day and sometimes he tells me things of interest from his day too. If my feelings were hurt at school, I can tell him or Mom when I go to bed. I notice I don't return to school the next day hating someone who hurt me. Telling Mom or Dad seems to free me of any hurt or angry emotions. It helps me to stay feeling good about the teacher and kids in my class.

If my behavior has resulted in some confrontation from the teacher or principal and my feelings got hurt in the process, I can tell my parents, and it helps me forget it and get to sleep. I notice I can go back to liking these people the next day too, instead of carrying more hurt and anger into the day. I feel sorry for kids who say they can't talk to their parents because their parents think their role is to give solutions, give advice, and give orders, or to punish a second time at home even if a child has been punished at school. All of this is parenting tradition. It's handed down through the generations. It's the beliefs that Chucky's parents go by.

No wonder my friends hide stuff from their parents. They are only going to get hurt more if they tell them things. My grandpa says the nation has turned back to discipline, discipline, discipline, the only answer millions of parents turn to in hopes that their kids will grow up right. He says conflict resolution skills of modern scientific psychology are still in their infancy and most parents have had no training to be effective and truly loving parents.

(Grandpa:) Sometimes a teacher will let parents know of some behavioral problem at school. When this happens, the parents need to become researchers with their child to get at the bottom of the problem. First the parents need to make sure they know what the problem is that the teacher is talking about. An exact description from the teacher needs to be followed by the parents describing what the teacher has said in a non-blaming tone. Then careful listening to the child for the child's understanding of what the behavioral problem is comes next. Here is where the listening skills come into play. Most parents don't know how to listen in this way. Once a thorough and accurate understanding of the problem has been described from both the schools' and the child's view, the parents can talk with the child about possible solutions, again in a non-blaming way. If the parents believe further confrontation of the child is needed, it can be done through descriptions to the child how the behavior might be bothersome to other students, to the teacher, or a concern for the parent, and why. The why of this is so important. This helps the child understand the effects of his behavior on other people and why it's important to figure out how to behave so others aren't negatively affected. All this can be done in non-authoritarian, non-blaming ways without accusations of badness, and without the use of punishment. Children will change behavior when simply talked to in these ways.

Punishment and removal of privileges or pleasures is imbedded in tradition and not at all necessary. Making kids feel they are bad is not a guarantee of improved behavior. The strong willed rebellious child can dig in to prove he can't be controlled out of bad behavior and embrace the behavior as a means of protecting his autonomy against adults. This is a habitual pattern no parents want and it's not going to lead to the child's success in the future.

Tight control is usually a part of treatment programs when a youth first arrives. It has to be used in early stages of treatment where control and over use of authority at home has led to habitual negative rebellious acting out. Unfortunately, by the time a child goes to treatment facilities for help, tight control is necessary to keep him controlled long enough for the therapeutic side to take effect. If the therapy is successful, the child will be able to function autonomously and responsibly, no longer in need of tight control. Those who don't take to the treatment will go out into the work world, the military or college highly unlikely to succeed.

(Dan: age thirteen) My Grandpa (Jan) was the psychological consultant for Youth and Shelter Services, a substance addiction treatment program for adolescents in Ames, Iowa, for ten years. He was also psychological consultant for Beloit of Iowa, a residential and outpatient children's treatment program in Ames, Iowa for ten years as well. Eventually he left the mental health center, went into private practice, and remained very busy until his retirement.

I don't want to leave the impression that very much of my life is wrapped up in fights with my brother or family conferences. I believe since my parents handle things in these positive ways, it greatly lessens my fighting with my brother. Family conferences are a rare occurrence, but they get us all back on good and solid grounds with each other when they are needed.

Most of the time my brother and I, at this stage of life, are having a ball. We're on the move with our friends all the time. Our parents are basically a taxi service. We are in ice hockey in the winter, soccer and baseball in the spring and summer. We do basketball camps in the summer and play basketball in the fall.

I love this life. Nothing could be more fun than sports with my friends and brother. We're constantly together. We ride vans and busses together across town or to the next town. I love these trips. My dad says I'm lucky to be growing up in a time where a little kid can have something to do for every season and get all these fun skills.

Since my dad, my mom, and my grandparents got me started into these kinds of abilities when I was young, I am in a good position to do OK in these sports with my friends. I feel sorry for my classmates whose dads or moms were not available, or whose dads or moms or grandparents didn't have these skills, except for those kids whose parents could teach them lots of other cool skills like dancing, music, theater, computer work, etc. Now that I'm in first grade, when we go outside for recess, I can hold my own with any of my classmates who love sports. We have fun, and I feel accepted and am valuable to the team. And academically I love school. I love to learn. I tell my parents about the interesting and exciting things I am learning each day at school. Unlike a lot of my classmates, I am at peace in the classroom. I'm not angry with the teacher's leadership. I enjoy the learning tasks. It's fun to feel competent and succeed at learning, just as it is out on the ball diamond. Some kids aren't into athletics, but are equally happy with other recess play and get involved in other pursuits that are equally as good for them.

My neighbor Chucky's dad was always busy and when they did get out in the yard to learn softball or soccer or basketball skills, it always went badly. Chucky's dad would get mad and go in the house, leaving Chucky outside feeling like he'd never be any good at anything. Because of the way Chucky was handled by his dad, he isn't any good at any sports. And I don't think he ever will be.

With all of these park and recreation sports, you'd think I'd not have time for fishing, or camping, or for days on Uncle Jerry's farm, or for piano lessons or for voice lessons or for painting classes. But surprisingly, I do have time for those as well. I even get time to disappear in the woods out back with my neighbor Chucky and other friends, sometimes for hours at a time. My folks say we are lucky to live in an area that is safe and where kids can have some independence and down time. Those times are some of the greatest. My parents let us enjoy participating in many of the park and recreation activities.

They let us do classes that we are interested in, but also insist that our schedules not be too demanding. They don't want us pressured too much in any skill development. They believe in letting kids be kids. They aren't out for perfection or great heights of achievements unless our abilities happen to take us there in a relaxed and enjoyable way.

God's Intention For Man Helped By Psychology: A Few Words From The Author Jan

(Author: Jan) Some churches think the word of God was total and complete in the scriptures alone. Others revere the BIBLE as an early revelation of man's developing understanding of God and go beyond it to tradition and science as sources of God's on-going revelation to man. I am finding myself in the second camp. It seems to me that God continues to make his will known to man. It took considerable development of more and more complex life forms for man with his ability to be conscious, free, and curious, to come to be. With each new century it seems science learns more and more about how God and the world functions.

My own Ph.D. is interdisciplinary, including both psychology and religion. I have a seminary degree, skill training to be a licensed psychologist, and a couple of more years in the areas of psychology and religion. After thirty six years of helping people for ten hours a day, I turn my hand back now to the Psychology of Religion side of my graduate studies.

I'm especially interested in what scientific psychology brings to the religions, now that it's had a hundred and more years of research. We have learned that no early societies could be found that didn't have some animism form of religion.[4] Religion has been around with man for at least 35,000 years.

Today psychology has discovered how to greatly improve parenting and family life such that the reality is here that we can help a loving God realize his wish for humankind. If God's

4 Marvin Harris Our Kind. NY: Harper perennial, 1989.

wish for people is to love one another, that love has surely had difficulty getting through due to traditional parenting behaviors. That barrier no longer needs to exist. Conceivably, God could finally spend a lot less time forgiving destructive and hurtful human behavior than he/she has ever had to do before.

If people grow up well loved in families, the priest could spend a lot more time celebrating the peace and joy of God in worship and far less time hearing confessions from a world that up until now seemed truly depraved. People have been deprived of love in families, so quite naturally it was easy for religionists to believe that human nature was depraved and evil. That's the way unloved people act.

The drama of people hurting one another is well documented in the Old Testament, as the lives of patriarchs, judges, kings and prophets all show. Abraham almost knifes Isaac to death believing God wants him sacrificed. Isaac and his mother steal the birth right from Esau. King David sends Bathsheba's husband to the front line to be killed so he can have her as a wife. The concept of forgiveness grows throughout the Old Testament as morally reprehensible behaviors had to be forgiven in the nation of Israel. It's not surprising that a concept of original and ongoing sin made sense as religions developed upon the planet. But I think it's time to modify that belief.

It is my experience that when people gain some skills in empathetic listening, self-disclosure, and consensus conflict resolution - all processes discovered by scientific research in the last two hundred years - that they can become the kind of parents who raise children who don't have to be destructive and hurtful to other people. I have witnessed good parents who raise good children and those children have never intended harm to anyone else. These are ambassadors of God's love in the world. The religion that incorporates these scientifically discovered skills and teaches them to their particular brand of believers will be making progress toward bringing divine love into this world.

Thirteen: Healthiness With School & Friends

(Dan: age thirteen) As I enter the teens, I think back to all the great times I had as an elementary kid. I love the all-out organized play of that stage. Sometimes my teammates and I were just into a run like you'd not believe. Seems like one thing goes right for one person and the next thing you know, everyone on the team is doing the most fantastic things. It's almost as if some higher power has moved in on our game and we're a bit out of this world in our play. Plays happened sometimes in these moments that were even a bit above our skill levels. It's hard to explain, but it really was true.

My grandpa says life seems to access another dimension sometimes. When I ask him what he means by another dimension, he says science is considering the possibility that there are dimensions beyond the five that we seem to have senses to know. When I ask: "Where is science looking for this kind of evidence?" He says they are looking at the atom. Apparently there are unexplained materials or substances in the atom that are not understood.

He says that there may be other universes than the one we know, maybe other worlds that could even be very near at hand, but our senses simply can't see or our brains know of it. I say to Grandpa: "Do you suppose we get a little help from these dimensions sometimes when everything seems to go right in a ball game?" Grandpa says: "Well, maybe."

(Grandpa:) Another way of saying the same thing is that perhaps some of the wonderful forces of these other dimensions, which could be God too, may draw closer to us at times than at others. Say given a boring old day where nothing much is going on, one might conclude that whatever exciting and wonderful energy we had in a great game seems to not be available to us. Maybe on those days we are quite far from this incredibly enjoyable thing that happens in great games when a team seems to go into a zone of some kind. Does the Eternal draw closer in some of our really great moments? How do we explain the energy of excitement? What about ecstasy? Are we helped by another world when we are having a great day? What happens when people are feeling close and loving after a good conversation? Why do churches use great choirs or great soloists? There is a concept in Positive Psychology that is taught in the most popular course ever at Harvard. This concept is called "flow". This is when a healthy person is enjoying something she really likes doing and the time just flies by. If we love our work, as I loved mine, we are in "flow". Buddhism has a concept called "mindfulness" when people are at one with what they are doing. They are clearly aware of the moment they are in and are completely absorbed in it. Would a loving God want for us to be in "flow" as much as possible in our lives?

When parenting is competent to provide security, stimulation, and closeness, the healthy child enjoys a lot of great moments in his life. Healthy adults remember their childhoods with fondness. They can remember, for example, moments of all-out-play with their parents, or grandparents or other children when the laughter and fun were at incredible levels. Does the Eternal come near in such moments?

Would skilled parenting allow for more of these than unskilled parenting? I think so. Who doesn't want a full and fulfilled life? We can do better.

(Dan: age thirteen) I like Grandpa's thinking. I feel so good when I'm around him and we are thinking of stuff like that. He seems to have such a positive view of life. I spend as much time with him as I can. I don't hear a lot of other people thinking things like that it seems. When we go fishing in his deck boat and the sun beats down and all is quiet, we have the greatest conversations.

There are other times I feel like I've gone a bit out of this world into something that feels mysterious and really, really good. I can hear songs that seem to elevate me to a feeling that I don't often get otherwise. These songs make me feel really lost in wonder and splendor. I've had these really moving moments with music as a kid, but I seem to have them a little more often now as a teenager. Grandpa says that growing up, he had songs like that. He said he felt strange and wonderful feelings with songs like *Canadian Sunset*. Of course, he's a snow skier as I am, and he loves to ski alone. He says he gets what he calls ecstatic by the end of a beautiful day in the mountains.

Other songs of Grandpa's that made him feel wonderful were songs that start with: "I have often walked on this street before" or "Once on a high and windy hill". I don't know these songs because they are really old. But I think I know what he's talking about. I'm really getting interested in girls now and I can have such a strong feeling that it would be wonderful to have a cute girl for my own. I could see life becoming almost out of this world. I like the fairy tales that end with "and they lived happily ever after." When Cinderella and the Prince finally got hitched up, I could see they were going to live in total bliss the rest of their living days, even if he did have to run a kingdom.

There is a really cute girl in my class that I am interested in. I like her personality and she's really smart. My folks say it's OK to ask her to a movie, so I think I will. Most of the time I just love hanging out with my group and she happens to be in the group. So we are already friends. I get near her every chance I can when the group is together and I think she is doing the same thing because we sure end up together a lot. That's what makes me think she'll say yes to going out.

I think I'll change the conversation for a bit back to the challenge of seventh grade. I am so excited about going to middle school that I can hardly wait sometimes. Some kids say they are scared of this big change of schools and all. I may be a little, but mostly I'm excited. I'm anxious to get on with it. It's got to be so neat to change classes to different teachers all day long and see the other kids in the halls like the big kids do.

Our sixth grade teacher warned us that there will be one colossal step up in homework when we hit seventh grade science. My folks have always pretty much stayed out of my schoolwork and I've always done well without too much effort. I've always gotten good grades, I think in part because my home is such a loving and stable place. My folks have never pressured me about academics. If I ever got into something very difficult, they were there to help me with it until I could start to master it. Then I'd be confident and back on my own.

Poor Chucky next door is smart as a whip, but gets rather mediocre grades in about half his subjects. I know he's just uncomfortably distracted most of the time. If a teacher gets a little strong with someone, he's all upset for days. He can get mad and wants to retaliate against teachers, the principal and the schools. If he gets any teachers in seventh grade who act a little over authoritarian, he's going to absolutely neglect his homework in that class. Everybody will wonder why he's flunking a class and getting high grades in others.

Chucky is kind of hostile at times to other kids. He isn't getting accepted very well in the group I like. Actually, no group is opening their arms to him right now. I hang out with him on the one-to-one especially in the neighborhood because I've always liked Chucky. I'm not going to abandon him now. I think I understand him better than most because I've seen him grow up next door. I think he feels safe and accepted by me and he isn't ever hostile to me.

I think he's looking up to the druggy kids. I'm advising him to stay away from them and follow his technological fascinations. I think he'd make a heck of an engineer, but he won't if he keeps flunking classes that are lead by teachers who get angry with some students once in a while. I keep asking him to see our guidance counselor, but he says his parents are against it. His parents are in a religious group now and they say the druggies are going to suffer in a lake of fire for eternity. I tell Chucky I don't think a loving God would torture anyone for an eternity. That sounds pretty hostile. But I tell him it would be good to give up drugs.

I tell him Jesus was facing death daily and was pretty angry with the religious leaders and the Romans for occupying and overtaxing his people. I tell him I think that's why he said those awful things about anyone who didn't believe and follow him. Or I say it's possible that the writers about Jesus a generation later may have wanted to scare people into believing and put those words into Jesus' mouth. I said most of the stuff Jesus said was pretty kind and loving to people. In other parts of the *BIBLE*, writers said Jesus said to "love your enemies", and if struck by someone, "turn the other cheek". I told him Nelson Mandela followed this side of Jesus' teachings when he got out of prison in South Africa and won the election, and set up a government cooperating with the very people who put him in prison. I tell Chucky not to sweat the idea of a hell, but Chucky seems worried sick over it. It's probably because he's hearing it every Sunday and Wednesday in his parent's church. But he doesn't seem interested in giving up drugs. I wonder if the drugs are an attempt on Chucky's part to have good feelings. I don't think he has much of the "flow" in his life that Grandpa speaks of. I wish Chucky could enjoy life like I do.

Let's go back to my challenge of handling seventh grade science. I've told my folks what my sixth grade teacher said about next year's science being a big step up. They told me not to worry because they would sit down with me and show me some of the study skills they figured out for surviving college. They told me once I had these skills to handle seventh grade science, I'd be set up for everything on through college and graduate school if I wanted to go. Right now I'm not thinking that far ahead. I'm mostly excited about middle school and high school. I think it's going to be so much fun to grow and learn and do sports and go to dances and participate in music at that level.

Sixteen: Healthy Choices

(Dan: age sixteen) I'm between my sophomore and junior years now and loving it. My parents got me started in seventh grade OK by teaching me some study skills with seventh grade science. Man, that book was massive and the memorization was the same. I haven't run into a course like it since. Maybe I never will again.

What they did basically was to tell me not to just read a chapter, but to take notes as I did so. They said to write down all the names or in the case of history, name and dates, that I'd have to remember. They said to go over these notes a few nights before tests and memorize them. It seemed like a simple thing to do, but what a difference it made when it came to doing tests. My grades are staying right up there and I'm happy for that because I want to do well. I like to do well academically. I like for people to think I'm smart and I'd like to not be limited in where I might like to go to college. The world out there is starting to look very interesting to me and I want to see what's out there.

I did ask out the girl I like. I was right about her wanting to stand around me back in our group when I was a seventh grader. When I asked her she said she'd like to go to a movie with me and would ask her parents. Apparently I passed OK with her parents because they said it would be OK.

She didn't live far from me, so we went to a movie on one chilly October evening. I guess in her excitement to get ready she forgot her gloves, so I lent her mine. I think she was pretty impressed with this gesture because she was willing to go to another movie a couple weeks later. From our very first date we seemed to be able to talk endlessly. Maybe in part, this was due to the fact that we were in the same social group and knew the same people. All I know was I enjoyed being with her and apparently she enjoyed being with me.

Now we are pretty well going steady. We go out twice a week and sometimes to ball games and such as well. There are some other couples we hang out with and sometimes we go out with the old group too, because we are still just kind of a big loving group. My folks, of course, sat down with me when we were first starting to go to movies. They said they'd recommend that I not have sexual intercourse with my girlfriend at the high school age. They said there could be a lot of expressing of affection without intercourse per se. They said nothing is more wonderful than an adult love relationship. They said that eventually expressing love through sex, of course, is a natural goal for people. They acknowledged that when one begins intercourse is a personal decision. They said it was my decision for my sexuality, but that their advice was to wait past high school anyway.

They said if I chose to start earlier than what they recommended, they would want me to use contraceptives for sure to greatly lessen the chance of an early pregnancy. They said that they wanted for me to be able to enjoy college years. They wanted me to be free to learn and have fun for many years before the responsibility of raising a child. I agreed with that and thought it made perfect sense. They said the reason they mistrusted contraceptives is that statistically there is still a 3% chance of pregnancy with them. That caught my attention. They advised me that "You really want to be financially capable before having any children. You want to have them when you are well prepared for them and want them." My girlfriend was in the same place, although we never really talked about it because it really didn't seem like an issue and we were both a bit embarrassed to discuss it.

We discussed what parts of the body we might not allow ourselves to explore at this age, so that neither of us would be uncomfortable with how we expressed our affection for one another. It was hard to talk about, but I truly didn't want her to think negatively of me or be uncomfortable. Once that line was drawn, we knew where each other stood and from then on we enjoyed considerable making out. We could express our affection for one another now in a way that was very comfortable. I'm glad my parents gave me guidance.

I'm finding my relationship with my girlfriend is another stable force in my life, as is my relationship with my parents. We both look forward to our dates and have a lot of fun together. We laugh a lot and always have a lot to talk about because of school and friends. We talk about our futures and who we might like to become and where we might like to go in the world.

Dating at first was an incredible high. Now it has smoothed out into what seems to be a secure identity. There doesn't seem to be anything to differ or fight about and we never really do. Our dates are simply the reward time of the week. We can talk endlessly and if we are upset by anything in life, we discuss it with one another. Actually we're both rather happy most of the time.

We are both really busy with sports, music, and academics. We are memorizing songs and plays and presenting constantly in class or elsewhere. Her parents have raised her much as mine have me. We are both happy with our parents and happy with school and one another. We are lucky in this respect, as we know a lot of couples who seem to be fighting all the time. They are breaking up and getting back together or going out with someone else on the side. They are in constant chaos. I think the conflict resolutions skills that I absorbed in my family are allowing me a really nice relationship already as a teenager. My relationship with my girlfriend is stable and rewarding instead of volatile and anxiety producing. I'm really glad for that.

Chucky has gotten into the druggy culture and groups. He has a girlfriend from that group. They both wear black and she has gotten into stealing I Pods from large stores. She distributes them out to friends. She has become rather popular for her courage and skillfulness as a thief. Interestingly, she doesn't steal from small family-owned businesses. She believes that large corporate America is somehow bad and deserves to be ripped off. Chucky hasn't done that, but he tells me of her new interest in stealing. He is considering it, but I'm advising him not to do it. He seems to listen to me. I hope he doesn't get into trouble.

He and his girlfriend are all fascinated with partying and stealing and hanging out with friends they hold in common. Chucky is so happy to have finally found a group of kids that accept him. His hostility now seems to be directed toward corporate America and he gets a kick out of people being offended and despising their dark clothing. They have a lot of metal on their skin. There are plenty of kids at school who wear black and facial metal who aren't stealing. Many of them are good kids. But Chucky has a number of teachers who dislike him and his dress. Other teachers seem to stay neutral about it and attempt to care about him and encourage him to stay connected to school. His girlfriend is already considering an alternative school because she isn't making the grade. Chuck himself is on the margin close to not passing. He is unwilling to consider any more time for his studies than just class itself. They both miss a lot of school. His parents are worried about his future and on him constantly, but he says he doesn't really care.

I am interested to note that Chucky reports a lot of conflict with his girlfriend. They seem to be in a control battle. She takes the position that I used to see in Chucky's parents, namely of controlling, judging, criticizing and getting mad a lot. Chucky still takes the position he did years ago returning home from a game with his dad. He cowers from her onslaught, feels bad, stays largely quiet and gets depressed. She has cheated on Chucky a number of times, but each time he takes her back again, though he feels pretty bad about it. They've been into early sex since about age 14 and have had two pregnancy scares. Chucky is strong into marijuana and alcohol and has tried methadone, crack and heroin on a few occasions. He has gotten violent at some of these parties. He owes landlords for broken doors and walls.

I'm suggesting to Chucky that he do a stint in rehab, as I believe he is already addicted. He listens to me, but I don't think he will turn it around, just yet. He says his art teacher and his theater teacher are both telling him the same things I am. He says he doesn't know why he behaves as he does. He seems to know it's not the way to go.

We all know Chucky is smart and has lots of ability. We tell him if he turns it around there is nothing that could keep him from succeeding in many directions in life. He tells me right now he really doesn't care about any of that. It all looks like work to him that would take him away from his friends and partying. I can see that he finally has friends and that's all that matters to him right now.

Sometimes I think of how it might be to become a psychologist like my grandpa and work with kids like Chucky. I wish he could understand what's happened in his life and let out all the hurt that's taken place in his growing up years. He could regain his birthright to become a happy and fulfilled adult someday and learn to be good to a wife, children and grandkids.

What a satisfying thing that must be if you could be a part of that kind of change in a person's life. My grandpa seems to be a very happy man. He feels good about what he's done in life. He glows with warmth, laughter and love. He has such a positive outlook on his own life and family. He's at peace with himself and dreams up all kinds of fun, either alone or with friends. He and Grandma seem so content together. They both seem to love people and are kind to everyone they meet. I hope I can be in a good place like they are when I'm seventy four years old.

One Giant Leap For Humankind:
The End of Teen Rebellion

(Author: Jan) Sigmund Freud himself observed the rebellion that was typical in teenagers of his day. Freud concluded that it was a normal part of adolescence. Sigmund Freud developed the theory of personality about having a superego (family and social values), ego (the thinker and self-regulator) and id (the emotions and impulses).[5] It would be later researchers who would discover the skills for how these ego states would work between individuals in relationships. In the mid nineteen hundreds psychologists discovered ways that parents could strengthen the ego (the self-regulating thinker) and no longer have to control the child from the parent's superego. This was a huge breakthrough in family psychology. It began to alleviate untold suffering.

With this discovery, now parents could be freed from parenting from a controlling superego. An awful lot of pain and suffering that used to be a part of society and families, namely religious and value fighting, began to fade away in favor of healthy and happy family relations. Parents began to understand that their child could hold values different from their own values. Their child could now choose a religious faith position different from his parents and still be lovingly close to them. Families no

---

5 Sigmund Freud Psychopathology of Everyday Life Dover edition, first published in 2003. (Translated by Dr. A.A. Brill). The Macmillan Company, New York: 1914.

longer felt that they had to abandon loved ones because they chose another branch of Christianity or another world religion. A protestant boy who fell in love with a catholic girl no longer faced rejection from his family for his choice of a mate.

People began to use their thinkers to evaluate their faith, instead of feeling pressured to blindly follow a religious viewpoint in order to please their communities of origin. The value of freedom of religion that had been incorporated in the nation's Constitution was beginning to become a reality in family life. The ecumenical movement within Christianity saw the beginning of calling off the mistrust that had waged conflict for centuries. Many societies and nations are trying to move toward tolerating differences. Jesus sensed this issue and asked people to not be judgmental with self-righteous intolerance. Traditionalists in the wings of most world religions are not yet turning this corner, and religious wars still plague the earth. But the hope is there for a future where all religions could be at peace. It's as if the seed has been planted and the arc of history is moving toward a better day for humankind.

But as brilliant as Freud's discoveries were, he didn't see yet that adolescents could be at peace with their parents. He thought they had to rebel to grow up and separate from their parents. For centuries society had assumed that authoritarian control by parents was the good way to parent. The result was that kids had to rebel to grow up or remain a child under their parent's thumb. This was the world Freud saw around him. He couldn't foresee that new developments in parenting could make rebellion a thing of the past. And, of course, not all of this is behind us yet. You can still hear, to this day, that "boys will be boys" as if drunkenness, high speed driving or promiscuity are simply part and parcel of normal teenage life. Too often when viewed this way, rebelliousness is expected, even unintentionally scripted by parents, and "winked at."

One of the unfortunate consequences of the authoritarian family culture was that generally parents always have wanted the best for their kids, but the authoritarian way always backfires for inculcating good values in the rebel kid. Behind the controlling parent belief system was usually a number of values that were good for kids, like safety, apply yourself in school, avoid early intercourse, and therefore pregnancy, and avoid promiscuity and therefore sexually transmitted diseases. In traditional parenting, the rebellious leaning teenager had to turn to some means to overthrow the control of the parent and, in so doing he overthrew good values in the process, and acted out dangerous behavior.

In order to demonstrate to the parent and the world that they are going to run their own lives, they far too often do behaviors that are opposed to their parents' caring and protective values. In Dan's case, he's a friend to his parents. He has good judgment. He listens to and follows his parent's caring advice because it is advice, not orders. He's self-regulating already. He applies himself at school because he wants to develop skills that express and show his abilities.

The adolescent's development of skills expresses his abilities and talents. This development during his adolescent years will be his life's pride and honor. One of life's primary purposes is to use our abilities. Eventually our abilities will be expressed in careers and hobbies which essentially become our contribution to the community around us. It's built into us to serve and meet the needs of one another. Probably life's greatest satisfaction is the ability to give to the community and to give successfully to the care and growth of your family through work. You generate money, but also do a good job by your children. You give them the opportunities they need to develop happily.

Notice the great drive on the part of the healthy adolescent to develop his talents and abilities in the teenage years. There may be some anxiety regarding, "How do I accomplish adult money generating capability?" But there is also an enormous and exhilarating drive on the part of most adolescents to do this. Especially this is true when they have had healthy development. If they have felt controlled or hurt, and betrayed by over-controlling parents, their development will not go well. Almost no matter how bad the parenting, there is usually some love for the parent along with the hurt and angry feelings.

Although love may faintly survive beneath the great parent child control / counter-control struggle, it isn't strong enough to stop the destructive effects of rebellion. For example, in Chucky's case, he doesn't really care about adult identity development. Subconsciously he knows that ignoring the developmental tasks frustrates his parents, and therefore he gets back at them. The longer he ignores vocational development, the longer he tortures his parents. Sometimes kids ignore this development well up into their adult years. This is a nightmare for any parent because most parents love their child. One of life's greatest disappointments is a parent watching his child chronically fail.

Modern psychology has learned that a child's ability to think is actually there from the beginning. With traditional parenting, pre-psychology culture simply lacked the knowledge and skills required to engage and access the thinker.

When Freud differentiated the superego (the parent pushing values on the child) from the ego (the child's ability to think, judge and decide), he planted the seed for future scientific discoveries. Modern psychology would go on to develop the skills to allow the child's thinker, and self-regulating ability, to grow. Once a parent learns how to talk ego to ego, or thinker to thinker with a child, and allows choice from the start, the child becomes self-regulating very early on. In the development, of self-regulation, the child develops self-confidence and self-esteem. By the teenage years, an individual with power, confidence and self-esteem can go through adolescence without what tradition thought was normal rebellion. None of my three kids showed any symptoms of rebellion.

They didn't need to drive at high speeds. They didn't need to use alcohol in excess. They didn't need to use drugs, steal from corporations or become violent.

So many of the behaviors that were viewed as normal teenage rebellion in the past don't occur today when parents know how to grow the thinker instead of grow resentment from early and persistent parental vigilance, over-teaching, preaching, and control.

If parents can trust and believe their children will grow up fine, the parents will be much more relaxed and easier persons to grow up around.

If the parents trust the future of their family's development, they will also convey a sense to their kids that they will grow up fine. This is called scripting. When a child catches from the parent that she will be a good and competent person, she is far more apt to become just that. If she senses from her parent that something in her development is going to go wrong, then it's much more likely to go wrong. If the parent is nervous, fearful, and pessimistic about the child's future, then the child herself will feel half out of control. The child, too, will believe she is not going to safely make it or become competent in life.

Parents who laugh at their child's mistakes or fumbling efforts to master things are sending a message of shame. This message is registered deep within the child that the child will not be competent. Such kids will approach the taking on of an identity in adolescence for adult preparation with a jittery sense that things always go wrong for them and nothing will work out well in terms of vocational success.

Along with this tendency in parenting is the fact that many parents will evaluate a child in the presence of others, not realizing that a child hears and records everything said around him from a very early age. If a parent describes a child negatively in some way, like in comparison to a sibling, that child will begin to act out the parent's description of him and so the scripting snow balls.[6] This child has a feeling she is out of control and on some negative pathway.

The self-regulating ego, or thinker, does not get unattached from these negative parental evaluations and it is ineffective against the script the parent has set up unknowingly. The more the child acts out the parent's evaluation, the more the

---

6 I first heard of scripting from Eric Berne Transactional Analysis in Psychotherapy Grove Press, Inc., New York, 1961.

parent sees and describes the definition to others in the child's presence, and this is how the die is cast. This child will not feel confidently in charge of himself.

This is in contrast to the parent who has a strong trust that his children will develop normally and well. One way a parent can develop that kind of trust is through education in child rearing. If a parent has some exposure to psychological skill development, he can feel much more confident about his parenting.

Education and training in parenting is one of those areas people seem to believe they won't need. I think they believe parenting will be a natural thing if they love their kids. Most all parents do love their kids. I imagine it's a very low percent of parents who give any time to learning to parent. By the time they see they are in trouble, untold damage has already taken place, like an undetected cancer. It's a very sad thing. Damage control is very painful and very expensive. If parents learn there is another way to parent, a way that science has discovered with skills that bring success in relationships, they can change the way they parent. To make that change, they need training in those skills. Once the skills are successfully acquired, they become second nature, and a lot of good can take place in a family.

Some families have come to believe that parenting education is essential. This has become a part of the culture of some of today's families. This new openness to education and training will only spread over time. Eventually human life on this planet will be improved by the science of parenting education. Future generations will have less heart ache, fewer divorces, less rebellion of teenagers, fewer addictions and less human tragedy. There will be more peace, happiness, fulfillment, contentment and success in human loving.

In chapters to come you will see how Chuck's life doesn't go well due to the harsh and strong authoritarian parenting of his parents. This book shows the worse results from traditional parenting. It illustrates the most severe example of harsh traditional parenting. Let me list the less severe results of milder forms of traditional parenting, where the loving side of parenting comes through in spite of the authoritarian methods:

Many normal adults who look perfectly healthy to most people none-the-less suffer the following results of traditional parenting:

1. Emotional pain throughout life.
2. Carrying low self-esteem feelings - the "I'm bad" feelings.
3. Can't fully believe in self.
4. Uncomfortable in groups.
5. Difficulty speaking up in groups.
6. Trouble being spontaneous, affectionate, fun loving or outgoing.
7. Not aware of the need to be close to spouse or people in general.
8. Overworked.
9. Unable to rest or slow down.
10. Not feeling safe throughout life.
11. Always somewhat anxious or emotionally down.
12. Trouble living up to one's potential.
13. Trouble getting in touch with emotions.
14. Couples getting upset with one another about which way to go in traffic.
15. Employees getting hurt and angry feelings when making group decisions.
16. Adults who always get bad feelings stirred up around their parents - having to ventilate negative feelings after visiting them so the love feelings can return.
17. Trouble making extended family decisions without getting into control struggles and hurt and anger feelings.
18. Families splitting up over inheritance issues.
19. Persons being too passive and easily controlled by others.

Late Adolescence - Early Adulthood:
Healthy Mate Selection

(Dan: age nineteen) I make my way to the door. In a minute she or her parent will appear and I may for the first time meet her parents. You could say I'm nervous, but I think that really it would be better described as excitement. What will they look like, I wonder? Will she look like her mother? Will she look like her dad? Will her parents look like they've taken care of themselves, or will they look burnt-out and somewhat defeated by life? Will I like her folks, or will they be a problem?

As luck would have it, she alone appears at the door, with that wonderful smile. Her folks aren't home. She is alone. My excitement and concerns about meeting her parents will have to wait for another time. It's probably a little premature to meet her parents anyway because I only met her a few weeks ago. And yet here I am at her door seeing her home for the first time.

I've been high now ever since I met her. As I came to her house, the song from the mid 1900's (that Grandpa taught me) came to mind: "I have often walked on this street before. But the pavement always stayed beneath my feet before. All at once am I several stories high. Knowing I'm on the street where you live". I've been into such an intense happiness from the day we first met.

I was simply heading into the library, where I hoped to get some material on tax exempt foundations for my paper in political science. I stepped up to the information desk and there she stood. I watched her a bit as she finished with another student. I was struck immediately with her cuteness. Her eyes sparkled. The tone of her voice was kind as she gave directions to the back stacks. She had a calm and competent demeanor. She was nicely groomed. Her hair was beautiful and she had a nice figure. I was drawn to her in a way that I had perhaps never felt with anyone before, even before saying hello. My high school girl friend and I had parted our ways in favor of meeting new people since we were going to colleges many states apart. Now I was off to college and loving it. It was such a great new stage in life.

Now she turned to me and smiled. She asked if she could help me. I wanted to say, "Yes would you be my bride for life?" But I knew that wouldn't be the thing to say, though it was strong in my mind. I told her about my research paper and asked how I might find the material I needed. She spent a few minutes on the computer and recommended a section to explore. She seemed to be intelligent in the way she did it. She said no one was behind me, so she could show me to the stacks.

When we got there, we each pulled references off the shelves. There seemed to be an undertow of happiness in our deliberations about our search. We both seemed to be enjoying one another's presence. I thought that if I were reading it right, she seemed to be as interested in me as I was in her. Unfortunately, we found quite a bit of good material, far too quickly as far as I was concerned, and she needed to get back to the information desk. I thanked her and she said, "Anytime," with a smile and was off.

When she was gone, I surmised whether perhaps she would be as nice and pleasant with any other library user and decided she probably would be. I couldn't help but wonder if she felt something special in my presence, as I did in hers.

I left the library and made my way to the Union for a coke, but couldn't get her off my mind. All I could think of was those few moments in the back stacks. The next day, of course, I found another pressing need for help at the library, and as fate would have it, being the exact same time of day and all she was there. This time, she greeted me with a less than business like "Hi". The "can I help you" again seemed the voice of some angel from a land yet unknown or explored by me. I described my new research needs and again she offered to accompany me to the information. Again the chemistry seemed equally as good. I was happy and relaxed and at-home in her presence, and she seemed to be the same.

When we were saying goodbye this time it seemed perfectly appropriate for me to ask her if she would have time, when she got off work, for a coke? Her words were again, as if uttered from Mount Olympus itself, "Yes, that would work for me". I was off and away, but deep inside there was immeasurable joy. And there it began.

I arrived at the library at the designated time and she completed a few details and grabbed her coat. Now I was actually walking beside her. This almost seemed too good to be true. We both seemed to smile a lot as we started the process of checking one another out. Where did we live on campus? Were we Greek or independent? What year were we in school? What were our majors? What teachers had we had in common? How did we like them? Where did we grow up, and on, and on. She had a sense of humor.

Much to our surprise, we simply frittered away the rest of the afternoon until the dinner hour. Unlike with some girls I had dated, the conversation seemed to flow so easily. Neither one of us seemed to want to part for the dinner hour, but we agreed upon our first date the following Saturday night, and went our own ways. I watched as she approached the exit door and she turned smiled and waved. She disappeared out the door and was gone again.

Time seemed to stand still in the next few days. I thought it appropriate not to show up to the library, although I wanted to every single minute. I watched constantly for her when I walked across campus, but never got so much as a glimpse. More than once I thought some girl was she, only to look again and see that it was imagination getting in the way of reality. I was so concentrated on my memories with her in those few days, as I waited for our first official date, that I forgot altogether what she actually looked like. So when she opened the door at her sorority, after Saturday evening had finally come, there was another explosion of perception, just to see her face. "Hi, how are you? Come on in".

This time she was dressed differently than she was at her library job. Her hair was pulled up. Her outfit was slightly more formal. She had jewelry which I hadn't noticed before, and there was color and definition from her make-up, that made her even more beautiful.

Again the evening came and went as if time were escalated. We went to a show, and when it was over, we made our way back to the Union, and again enjoyed a coke and some pie. Once again the talking flowed as if we had known one another forever or perhaps in some previous life. We settled into a dating relationship which we both seemed to continue to enjoy with no particular setbacks or difficulties. The more each of us knew about the other, the more we simply concluded that this was meant to be. We each talked of feeling like the other was the person we had been looking for, from early in our mate selection memories.

The semesters came and went, as did our regular dates. On some later visit to her home I met her parents, and she met mine. Our parents seemed happy enough with our choices and we soon became staples in each other's families. She looked like a combination of her parents. Neither presented me with any particular roadblocks or problems. They seemed to like me. I had a lot of similarities to the looks and temperament of her father, and it wasn't at all hard to understand the mate selection drives in her choice of me.

I couldn't see my parents in her, as they say in mate selection theory, but who knows? After all, love is blind. I always had a weakness for short brunettes whereas my mother was more a medium height brunette. Both my grandmothers were short brunettes come to think of it. This girl had spunkiness and a sparkle, which much too often I had heard was a characteristic of my mother. She also was endowed with a lot of common sense and organization, which has served overtime to keep my idealistic and imaginative feet on the ground. That sounds more like the attraction of opposites that folk legend describes, and psychology agrees, is in the mix.

All I know is that I was always attracted back to her to talk. That seemed fundamental to my emotional well-being and her personality, intelligence and physical beauty made the whole thing a slam-dunk. I was committed without ambivalence or question. It felt like I could spend endless hours with her simply frittering away time, were such an abundance of time possible.

(Grandpa:) Of course, at age nineteen, time together was never abundant, nor should it be. Nineteen is a busy time for identity development. And time together would not be abundant at least until retirement years later. But those retirement years were to become the crowning point of intimacy, beyond Dan's wildest dreams of possibility on earth. Finally, years later, they would be able to spend most days idling away time in one another's company, sprinkled in with a few friend and family contacts, and wonderful ample time to simply follow their own preferences and desires.

As life proceeds over time, if love goes right, quantity of sexual enjoyment is replaced by quality in an ever-growing marvel of physical fulfillment, again beyond any adolescent or young adult imagination. Today research is finding that even the quantity doesn't vary a whole lot. Young adults seem to think that surely they must have the sexual upper hand, being new at it and full of hormonal drive. It will come as a pleasant and welcome surprise that deeper and deeper satisfaction and fulfillment will mark the road to the golden years and beyond. That is, of course, if love goes right.

(Dan: age eighteen) I was in a pretty good position for such a positive life development story due to the kind of parenting that I was fortunate to have received. Not everyone is so lucky. Consider ole Chucky, now better known as Charles. While my adolescent and young adult mate selection activities went largely free of turmoil and trouble, Charles's experience, wasn't so good.

(Grandpa:) Within weeks of his first dating experience Charles was in a power struggle. His first relationship was stormy. Not only was he feeling controlled from practically the outset , but also he wanted to spend far too much time with her. All the activities Charles should have been doing, like being organized, spending time on skill or knowledge development, and carving out identity, were sacrificed for being with his girlfriend.

He managed to select a girl who had a strong critical and controlling parent in her head who matched to a tee his father's temperament and demeanor. She had a rigid right and wrong about her as well, and very soon began to point out to Charles where he was failing. Her pointing out his flaws is actually a healthy stage in a relationship and it can serve to improve the relationship, by helping each person grow away from his or her flaws. Starting feedback happens after people are together a while, but Chucky heard it as control and thus couldn't use it and benefit. She expressed it in controlling ways unfortunately. She had a strong but inflexible insistence on her way, and lacked any ability to listen to his side when differences occurred. This matched Charles's inability to speak up for himself given the overbearing nature of his father's communications..

While her tendencies weren't exactly good for Charles, and he became very uncomfortable very soon, it did feel familiar to him, like old home week apparently. He was ready to ride that horse whether it was happiness producing or not, because it was what he knew. Life continued on as it had been for him. He knew nothing else. And somehow, unbeknown to the average person, old parent child patterns of communication are a powerful mate selection draw. It's the Myth of Sisyphus, it seems, tragically enough. The person pushes the heavy ball up the ramp and when it approaches the top, it gives way and slides to the bottom. The person painfully jumps out of the way and proceeds back down to start the push and the climb all over again.

If Charles could have only gotten some therapy along the way, he may have been saved from the horrible chain of being that he had been born into, and continued to play out. But, of course, any notion of seeking out modern psychology would have been condemned by his family value system. A religious world view of two to three thousand years ago was authority enough for Charles's family, and modern science was to be avoided at all costs. And, of course, the costs described here for Charles are tragic as he continues to carry the chains of family pathology, passed down through the generations.

The Twenties, Thirties, & Forties: Healthy Marital Love Deepens: How To Stay Close

(Dan: age twenty-five) Our relationship continued well as we settled into our married twenties. The strong romantic love feelings gave us a good foundation for our marriage. I think more than that was the growing emotional bonding that was to spring from endless conversations about life. In the early stages we couldn't get enough time just talking about life, its meanings, our values, our past and our hopes for the future. Some of this undoubtedly was a testing process, to see if our values were enough alike to make for a wise marital choice that could afford reasonable compatibility.

From the start I found I could talk with her very easily, whereas sometimes in previous dating, the conversations didn't seem to flow so smoothly. Once we were married, we began the adventures of continuing graduate education, and eventually making a living. The schedule then most necessarily pulled us apart into our separate identities and separate worlds for much of our day. We would return to one another, however, anxious to share dynamics, the insights, the anxieties and the conflicts of our time away from each other.

(Grandpa:) It was in these daily discussions that the real bond of love deepened. This was beyond physical attraction and romantic zeal. This would be the true cement of their relationship, the bond that would hold them together for a life time. Having someone who you can see daily, to process all the emotions of life, becomes the greatest deep-down-inside satisfaction of intimacy hunger. The weather can be horrible outside, hot, cold, rain, snow or sleet, but being tucked away in one's home, be it an apartment in the early graduate school days, or city, or a country home later, shut away from the world and its stresses, will always be the best feeling. The deepest hunger for human intimacy is met in a relationship where people can share openly, honestly and deeply of their inner-selves.

If this takes place successfully in a relationship, a couple will be ready to handle whatever life throws at them, and yet stay together and be happy. If people don't grow up with this kind of deeper sharing of emotions in their family of origin, they are much more apt to not develop it in their adult love relationship. People can come together due to romantic and sexual attraction in their early adult years but never grow into this kind of emotional intimacy. Their relationship will be at risk with the stresses that will come over time with job and family.

The romantic and sexual attachment requires this deeper talking emotional intimacy in order to survive and stay fresh and dynamic over time. Without it, people lose sexual interest and are thus vulnerable to extramarital attractions. The mate selection motivator starts up outside the marriage, and most often divorce is the only seemingly reasonable consequence.

Dan was fortunate to have had openness of sharing emotions in his family, as was his wife. People tend to select a partner who has the same patterns as they had in their families. If a family is defended against emotion, a person will be uncomfortable with a potential spouse who is open to emotion. If a family is open to emotion, their members will seek a partner who is open to emotion. I think comfort or discomfort with emotion, and deep talking, is the single biggest factor in mate selection.

For couples who start out without emotional intimacy capability, trouble very often starts in a year or two. The romantic feelings run out without it, and people very early start to lose interest in their partner, and start looking around again.

Success comes from other dynamics as well, and those are the capabilities of conflict resolution. It's the family of origin that determines a newly attached couple's patterns.

If the family of origin lived with patterns of dominance and submission, and patterns of emotional distance, these patterns will also be involved in the mate selection dynamics. In families with dominance and submission patterns, some siblings will be aggressive and dominant, while others will be passive and dependent. When these individuals get old enough to date, they will find someone the opposite of themselves. A passive sibling will seek out a dominant partner; a dominant sibling will seek out a passive partner. You add romantic and sexual attraction to patterns that fit, and a relationship is born. If the dysfunctional patterns are not recognized, and worked on, a whole new generation will repeat the pathologies of the past generations.

In families like this, the parents will each represent an opposite pole; the dominant spouse will be in conflict with aggressive children, and the passive spouse will avoid conflict, as will the passive children. When individuals in their dating and mate selection pick out the opposite, these patterns will not change unless troubles create pain that leads someone to seek out knowledge about what's happening, and then patterns can start to change.

As Dan moved into his early adult years, he no longer saw a lot of Charles, as their adult identities took them in different directions. Charles had attached to a girl late in his adolescence, who, he told Dan, "turned out to be too bossy." Charles said: "Since I was sexually attracted to her, I remained in the relationship far longer than I should have and things got ugly."

Charles's substitute for emotional depth and intimacy was his addictions. He had taken up with drug involved kids, partying many nights a week late into the nights. He wasn't functioning in high school and got off in an apartment with other drug involved kids and got himself a fast food restaurant job. Like him, some of the others would have jobs for a while and they'd pay the rent. But no one sustained jobs because staying drunk and high at nights didn't bode well for getting to work in the mornings. And they were constantly getting kicked out of their apartments for not paying the rent.

Although Charles and his girlfriend had met at drug and alcohol parties, and enjoyed being high together in the beginning, more recently these parties turned into drunken fights between them. Charles describes too many times when his drug and alcohol use resulted in temper outbursts where he would punch holes in screens and walls. This would happen during fights he was having with his girlfriend after both were living together with the group. While Charles was passive when sober, he was prone to the same kind of temper outbursts as he had seen his father do in the home growing up. He said his anger seemed to come from moments of wanting some say or control and not being able to get what he wanted.

Charles's parents had disowned him when he left home and had very little contact over recent years, which Charles said was fine with him. He said getting away was good and he really didn't seem to miss them, which would be true because they were not deeply and emotionally bonded.

(Dan: age thirty) When I last saw Charles, he told me he had his third drunken driving charge, and also faced domestic violence charges for having hit his girlfriend in a drunken stupor. He explained that he had been court ordered into extensive chemical dependence treatment and that it had been extremely uncomfortable for him. Besides being weaned away from street drugs and alcohol, he had been badgered night and day to open up to his deeper self and his real emotions. He said it was like being asked to do something he had never known before. He saw others open up and sometimes cry for days before finally getting all the pain out. All the history of their conflicts with their parents poured out with great emotional pain. The pain had been sealed up since early childhood and was seemingly a bottomless pit. Charles said that for whatever reason, he never could do that.

Even though Charles didn't open up as the therapist in the treatment program had hoped for, he was able to maintain sobriety after the treatment program. He was introduced to the treatment philosophy to acquire a faith for a higher power. When he finished the treatment he wasn't attracted to mainline Protestantism or mainline Catholicism, but was attracted to literally interpreted *BIBLE* centered large gatherings of Christians.

He explained that he liked the idea that God had the power to help him maintain sobriety. He didn't feel he could do it himself. He liked the large worship services and the music. The church provided him with lots of large group human contact since he no longer had the drug involved community to get high with. He says he badly needed a philosophy that he could be forgiven for all his past. He could now get a fresh start in feeling good about himself in spite of all he had done. He said he needed the rigid rules of good and bad and the threat that he would not get eternal life unless he stayed sober. The idea that the devil had gotten a hold of him and made him do what he had done to himself and others helped him feel better about why he had done it.

(Grandpa:) Since he grew up in a black or white, right or wrong, household with a lot of control and criticism of him as bad, he felt at home with the black and white, right or wrong values of the conservative wing of Christianity. The emphasis of being good now instead of bad was helpful to Chuck and gave him support to stay sober and away from the so-called bad friends whose togetherness was based on getting high and rebelling against society. The new high of church worship seemed to fill in for the lost highs of drugs and alcohol partying.

Charles had beat his addictions with treatment and the help of conservative religion, but his relationships continued to not go well. He hadn't really succeeded in treatment to open up and heal the great anger and hurt left over from his childhood. He still couldn't handle the stresses of every-day married life with children. The frustrations would uncork his anger, and his model for parenting which was his overly harsh father was repeated in his own angry and overly critical approach to his kids. It is as if what he knew deep down was wrong about his father's parenting, when he was a kid, now was repeated in his own parenting, as if now he believed that his father had been right

It seemed to him the only problem was that he had been a rebellious kid and now he would do just as his father had done. If his kids didn't immediately submit and obey on cue, they were bad kids. The woman he did marry after a number of failed dating relationships left him for the good of the kids, but also had lost her love for him due to the angry control battles. She also complained of loneliness within the marriage. She said the relationship was lacking in zest and close intimate conversations. She had lost sexual interest in him. She no longer wanted to be around him much less be his wife. She wanted herself and the kids to be as free of him, as possible. Chuck was failing to meet the emotional and sexual needs of his wife. She took the kids with her when she left him.

(Dan: age thirty three) My love relationship continued to grow. The control battles that Charles was experiencing in his relationships never developed in our love relationship. Our communication remained close and warm and we compromised our conflicting wants and needs. After living together for a while, we each felt some resentments about our partner, but unlike Charles and his partners, we could openly express these resentments, and each of us grew from the feedback. We took it as constructive criticism rather than thinking it was any attempt to control. By addressing resentments our personalities grew and changed for the better. This enabled our love to remain and grow deeper.

Unlike Charles, we weren't comfortable with the new wave of conservative religion. The emphasis on good and bad, right and wrong, devil or angels, and literal interpretation of the scripture didn't appeal to us. Neither of us felt we had mistreated ourselves, or anyone else, in our development. The idea that we were sinners through and through that required constant forgiveness just didn't seem to fit. Or the idea that we needed some radical change away from bad behavior simply didn't ring true.

We both had been good to our parents, our friends and the authorities in our development. We bonded to and liked our teachers. We were glad to follow their suggestions and meet their expectations and do our homework. We enjoyed the process of learning, finding many of our subjects exciting and fun to master. Overly harsh or negative authorities we simply worked around. We didn't get hooked by them and hurt ourselves by not doing their assignments, as if to get back at them. We simply didn't have the big hurt and anger inside us that Chuck carried due to his conflicts with his father. Negative teachers, therefore, didn't set off rage and revenge feelings. Grandpa says Charles's desire not to succeed was motivated in part to frustrate his father who like all parents wanted his child to be successful. Grandpa says Charles' father didn't have the skills to raise a successful, strong, confident and happy child.

Neither of us had ever used destructive behavior on others or ourselves. We both stayed on track with meeting academic requirements and chose higher education as a means of preparing ourselves for a good financial future. The satisfaction of establishing a love relationship and preparing for a good career was fulfillment and excitement enough for us. Excessive alcohol usage or drug use didn't appeal to either one of us. We were happy with life as it is. Our parents encouraged and complimented us. They gave us a sense that we would, of course, succeed. It was simply a given. We were happy in the presence of our parents growing up and we expected to be happy as adults. Our parents' relationship, when we were growing up was loving, successful, and stable, and we simply expected to have a similar adult love relationship.

Neither one of us was interested in getting drop dead drunk or being constantly stoned. We were happy enough being sober and clear minded. Neither of us was full of anger that invited rebellion against society, as Charles was. We both enjoyed good relationships with our parents and stayed connected with them. We called them often and visited them regularly. We wanted to be present for the larger family gatherings of uncles and aunts and cousins because we found those relationships rewarding and enriching.

Our relationship began not by sharing drug or alcohol highs, as Charles's had, but simply conversations about life, and about our experiences in our worlds when we were apart. My grandpa says one definition of love that he liked was: "Always being anxious to get back together and talk." And this was true for us, whether our being away was for a day of our professional lives to return in the evenings, away for a week to professional meetings, or perhaps someday in the future in our retirement, when we will be away a few hours to see our own individual coffee groups.

We always look forward to talking upon our return to our home and one another. Grandpa would say if couples aren't experiencing this, their relationship is at risk.

(Grandpa:) For couples who have this emotional intimacy at the heart of their relationship wild horses can't pull them apart. They are the ones who grieve deeply and profoundly at the loss of a partner by death. They are the ones who retain a dynamic and fulfilling sexual relationship, throughout their years together. They are deeply bonded to one another. This quality in an adult love relationship is precious for those who have it. It keeps marriages happy, individuals physically and mentally healthy, and is bedrock for raising healthy, happy children.

(Dan: age thirty-five) The emotional bond that my wife and I had in our early years gave us a means of processing any emotions that surfaced in our lives either together or apart. Unlike the great-submerged boiling and suppressed anger and hurt that Charles carried, our emotions were more appropriate to the reality events of our lives. If our feelings got hurt at work with colleagues or bosses, or clients and students, we would process these hurt or angry feelings when we got time in our day's schedule to be together. Our hurt and anger was mild, and appropriate to whatever the issues were that created them. Charles's emotions were much stronger than what the reality stimulus should evoke.

(Grandpa:) After getting out the hurt, anger, guilt, or fear that may have been created during our day by talking with our partner, we return to loving and happy feelings while also getting ideas for returning to the situation and coping with it. When we return to the people we work with, we are equipped to handle and resolve conflicts and issues rather than risking strong bad feelings festering and blowing up delicate work dynamics. Strong negative emotions can fester, blow up in the work place and alienate colleagues and threaten job security. Charles' resume reflected many job changes, not due to recurring improved opportunities and better jobs, but to constant conflicts, firings, and abrupt leavings of damaged and seemingly impossible work relationships. Over time he had less and less opportunity to advance his career.

In our culture there is a commonly heard adage to never bring home your work conflicts. This would be true for people who would bring bad feelings home from work and spread them onto the family in a scapegoating way. But it shouldn't mean to never talk with your spouse about your work. An open caring and loving spouse is always open to his partner for dealing with her issues in the work world. To hide such pain from each other is to not be close to each other. People need ventilation of their work feelings with a caring partner.

Whenever a partner is hurting about something, he needs to talk with a caring spouse who can be a quiet, caring, responsive listener. The only way this happens is that each partner has a certain conviction deep inside. That is that each believes that his partner is smart, capable, and has a good problem solving rational process within her. Only with this belief can a person be a good listener to his partner's problems and his partner's pain.

Only with this conviction can we be confident, attentive and receptive listeners. If we thought our partner was deficient in some way, we would take on ourselves the responsibility of solving her problems. Now instead of it being her problem, it's our problem. Instead of letting her get out the painful emotions and brainstorm for solutions, we think we have to provide solutions and solve the problem. Thus in this way, unknowingly, we shut her off and up, and start giving advice.

There is always a first stage for listening to another's problem. That is, to be comfortable while the other person gets out all the painful emotions, like guilt, or anger, or sadness, or fear. If the partner seems a bit irrational in this first stage, that's fine. Because to get out pain, sometimes we need to overstate it a bit, maybe blame others unfairly, and carry-on a bit. This releases the painful emotions. If we stay attentive, receptive, and caring, and accepting of these so-called irrational emotions and viewpoints, our partner can get them out of his system, out of his body, and off his mind. Traditional parenting is afraid of emotions. Children are taught to "not complain, to keep a stiff upper lip, to be strong" and certainly not to express emotional pain. The reason for that is that generations have had these emotions repressed. It has been the role of traditional parenting to drive emotion into repression. Hence children's emotional pain threatens to uncork the suppressed emotional pain that the parent had in her childhood. So the parent can't be comfortable with the children's open emotions.

To change this around, parents need to work through their own repressed emotions, after which they can now be comfortable hearing their children's emotions. Learning to label what's going on inside is an important new discovery. Mankind has probably done it for centuries, sometimes well, and sometimes not so proficiently, but scientific knowledge about its importance is only about seventy years old. Searching for and sharing one's emotions are the greatest sources of partner intimacy. How to do it well is one of the great breakthroughs for humankind. The general population can benefit greatly from the knowledge of how to positively express emotions.

Charles explained to Dan that he just couldn't stand his wife talking about her bad day, whether from home with the small kids, or whether from her office. It just upset him too much. He would convey there was something wrong with her to have such difficulties. If she were an OK person, she wouldn't have all these bad feelings in life. Charles's wife soon learned that he wasn't going to be a sounding board for the tough things in her life. If she were going to talk to anyone at all about her pain, it would have to be a girlfriend, or maybe some male friend in her environment.

It is such attachments to others that may lead to the birth of romantic feelings or extramarital attractions. It can lead to the beginnings of a new mate selection process. Many affairs are symptoms of a marriage that lacks emotional closeness. People in affairs often say, "I could talk to that new person. I couldn't talk to my husband or wife anymore." If the need for emotional closeness isn't met at home, it will invariably pop up somewhere else in the environment. Sometimes people will be closer to their friends for actually processing their pain and issues, and simply live with a marriage that is emotionally distant. Sometimes one parent attaches this need to talk and be emotionally close to a child, since he or she doesn't get it from a spouse, and that places a burden on a child. Sometimes this child has trouble attaching to friends or a lover because she senses her parent is emotionally dependent on her. So she feels, on almost a subconscious level that she shouldn't leave the parent and grow up.

(Dan: age thirty eight) Early in our marriage we discovered what Grandpa meant about listening comfortably to the first stage, the so-called irrational stage. Letting one another ventilate without cutting this stage off with advice of some kind keeps my wife and me coming back to talk about our day. Grandpa says the biggest mistake is that when the listener takes on the burden of being the problem solver, he is unable to listen to pain. He inadvertently cuts off his partner's healing ventilation of irrational emotions. A belief that the partner will access her own thinker to come up with solutions helps him not get into the: "Here's the answer to your problem," "Here is what you should do." Grandpa says you should listen in an interested and caring way to the ventilation of the emotions involved in the situation. Then let the partner generate ideas for solving it with her own thinker.

He says cutting off the partner's talking and sending solutions too early are the two biggest blocks to marital intimacy.

Partners often give up in despair of talking with each other. They know something doesn't feel good, and what doesn't feel good is their partners are trying to solve their issues instead of listening with a caring tone. They want to prevent their partners' pain in the situations instead of letting them feel their pain, get it out, then move onto their own solutions. The impulse is a good one, namely to help their partners, but the good intentions do no good when the skills for listening are lacking. The partners will not get through the first stage of sharing a problem. Instead, they will know it doesn't feel good and close off, and go away with all the emotions still stuck inside.

(Grandpa:) If people know all of this, the one needing to talk can signal her partner that he has taken over again instead of listening. Then a partner who is starting to learn this skill can say, "Oops sorry, I did it again. Please proceed and I will shut up and listen to you. Please forgive me". A knowledgeable person who needs to talk can let her partner know what's happening. The listening partner can resume a caring listening posture instead of interfering in the process. When people get skill training and begin to feel competence in meeting their partners' emotional needs, there is a great relief. Safety feelings set in about their relationships. And excitement about their love and their future begins to replace confusion, failure, and dying love. Unfortunately, just reading this may not be enough. If you don't have these skills, get into a class for couple communication. It's a good investment toward a future of a happy marriage and a happy family. What could be more important?

This phenomenon is the number one biggest reason for marriage failure. People seem to shake their heads in bewilderment as to why so many marriages fail, as if there is no answer. There is an answer. The solution is in the training of people in listening skills, probably at the middle school and high school level. By now you may be asking, "What are these skills? How do you listen in a way that allows the first stage to get resolved in a healthy way? How do you listen comfortably to mild or strong negative emotions in a way that allows a partner to get those feelings out of his system? How do you keep from cutting him off with caring advice?"[7]

If you grew up in a family that was uncomfortable with emotions, and learned to put one another down if such emotions were trying to surface, you would continue to do so in your marriage. Education that described such emotions as good instead of bad would be the starting point. Practice in getting comfortable with your own negative emotions would be required. Once you could do that, then learning skills of how to clarify your partner's negative emotions - instead of condemning the emotions as bad or avoiding the emotions by giving advice - would be the remaining tasks to master. The skill of clarifying emotions requires that you remain neutral about the feelings. You need to communicate to the person that it is OK for her to feel whatever she feels, and wait silently for her to continue. This will help her go deeper into the issue and her feelings. This is the opposite of doing something that requires her to stuff it all back down inside.

Clarifying emotions involves an asking if this is indeed the emotion or the idea she is trying to express. This is done in a caring voice instead of with irritation that conveys discomfort, like "I don't really want to hear this." Or, "I can't take this. Please get off the subject, or get on with it, and get on to something positive." I am describing emotional education here. Have you ever heard of such in an American school curriculum? Have you ever wondered why math, other sciences, English, history, all are so much more important? Interpersonal relationship skill training could save so much relationship failure in our society both in the home and workplace, not to mention the enormous suffering that people go through. Also consider the drag on the tax dollar that unsuccessful relationships bring into medical and mental health costs.

---

7 I give credit to Carl Rogers and his research. I was first introduced to listening skills in graduate school at Boston University: Rogers, Carl R. Client-Centered Therapy: Its Current Practice, Implications, and Theory. Boston: Houghton Mifflin, 1951.

The psychologically scientific skills for listening and talking have not gotten out into the majority of society. Most people today are communicating the way their parents and grandparents have communicated, and are raising their kids the way their parents and grandparents have raised kids, for centuries. Thus the same social ills and problems continue to be passed down through the generations. A lot of suffering, both psychological and physical, can be attributed to this lack of skills for the world citizen, American or anywhere else.

Since I have promised you a deeper analysis of the skills of adult love relationship conflict resolution - which I'll do in the next three chapters - I want to have Dan remind you of how he absorbed these skills from his parents when he was a child.

(Dan: age forty-five) Fortunately my wife and I had absorbed healthy listening skills from our families. Our families were already adept at talking about daily stressors in order to get support with their worlds. Negative emotions were allowed us from birth on instead of repressed in our infancy, our toddler years, and our pre-school years. Our parents used talking and listening skills to deal with the conflicts of toddlers and preschoolers. They, and their parents, (unlike their grandparents) had gotten skill training from psychology, social work, and education curricula in college. They didn't deal with difficult child emotions by labeling frustrating behavior as being bad.

When I was a preschooler in conflict with my sibling over a toy, my parents would referee instead of label and order. For example, they would provide the structure to talk and listen. They would say to my sibling: "What's happening? Why are you fighting?" in a neutral voice. They then had my sibling describe her side of the conflict. Take the classic one: "He took my toy," (Said with anger and perhaps tears).

They would say something like: "You were playing with your toy and your brother took it from you?" They would say this instead of the traditional way of the parent being frustrated and angry. In the traditional way they would look for who was bad and perhaps punish one of them. They, the parent, would decide who was to play with the toy – i.e. send a solution.

Unlike tradition, our parents would get one child's story out in the open and be accepting of whatever the emotions were. Then they would do the same for the second child: "So, Dan, what is your side of it?" This, again, was done in a neutral and caring tone of voice. You would expect the usual blaming of the sibling, like, "He's had the toy for a long time, and I like it too, so he should share it, etc." Again, this is probably stated and overstated with hurt and angry emotions. The parent accepts these emotions as OK. And after both sides have ventilated their usually somewhat irrational and strong feelings, our parent would proceed with clarifying the conflict. "OK Jane wants the toy, and Dan wants the toy. We have a problem. Does anyone have an idea how we can solve this problem?"[8]

Since we children have gotten the emotions out that drove the conflict, we would access our own thinkers and come up with a solution. Now that the strong emotions had been accepted, and no one was labeled bad for having these emotions, the chances of a mature and rational solution were much better. Now one of us could see a more mature way to solve it, like one child being willing to give in and lose, and letting the other have it. Or sometimes we'd suggest a time solution, like one play with it another five minutes and then let the other play with it five minutes.

(Grandpa:) You will notice here that Dan described the same way of resolving a conflict as a child as I'm suggesting you do in your adult love relationship. If you've learned it as a child you will have a much smoother adjustment to living and cooperating with your adult love relationship. If we had universal relationship skill training, it could be one giant psychological leap for humankind.

While the world is proud of technological progress, and greatly benefiting from it in so many ways, the world largely

8 I first heard of this repeating of both sides, then asking for a solution from Tom Gordon, Parent Effectiveness Training: Three Rivers Press. New York. Copyright 1970, 1975, 2000.

remains depressed and befuddled about any potential social progress for humankind. There is a pessimism about social progress. The world feels out of control on this matter. The benefits of psychology are still hidden from the world. The profession has been swallowed up in the treatment of the mentally ill, and money for prevention and education of psychological skills for normal people has not become a priority, yet. When it does and when it becomes integrated in our education system, new confidence for solving social problems will be a big relief. The world will no longer feel helpless about the future of social problems.

(Dan: age fifty) Thankfully, due to our parents having ended the ways of centuries of tradition, we grew up with good self-esteem, and skills for getting along successfully with people. No wonder our marriage started out smoothly and stayed loving and tranquil.

In the chapter to follow, my grandfather gives you THE MODEL FOR HANDLING RELATIONSHIP DIFFERENCES that he gave me when I started to date girls, and I've gone by it ever since.

A Model For Handling Relationship Differences

(Author: Jan) I believe everyone grows up in his family with a slight, moderate, or strong tendency to be either too yielding when in conflict with other family members, or too unyielding. Over time every individual will need to become aware of his own tendency and correct it. When he successfully corrects it, he acquires the middle road ideal of being both appropriately assertive in conflict, and yet empathetic to the other person's view, so that differences can be smoothly handled in adult love relationships.

Many times these two types of individuals select each other in their mate selection because they won't be comfortable with their own types. This pattern then finds one person unable to express **all** the thoughts and feelings he has inside when he is in conflict with his partner. Instead, he sees rather intuitively the other's needs, wants, and views, and yields automatically, without even exploring openly his own side of it. The other person, the too unyielding person, can express her needs and wants and values when in conflict, but does not want differences, and tends not to be very empathetic (i.e. understanding of her partner's view), and does not invite his full expression. This relationship then proceeds with a higher satisfaction level for the one than the other, over time. Usually, in my experience as a marital therapist, it is the more passive partner who will begin to lose his original love feelings over time. People simply can't be controlled. If they are, they won't be happy and won't retain love feelings for the controlling partner.

Over time in a relationship, individual growth and development may take place. Often the passive partner begins to get stronger and may begin to move up into what I call the second stage of development. He gets a strong desire to be more in charge of himself and his destiny. All of a sudden he wants to meet his own wants and needs, better than they have been met before. Typically, he begins to demand his own way. He develops a strong fear of being controlled, and begins to receive his partner's expressions, when in conflict, as if he will surely be controlled. The strong feeling that develops is best expressed by this sentence: "YOU WOULD GLADLY MEET YOUR NEEDS AND WANTS WHEN WE DIFFER, AND LEAVE MINE UNMET." Since his stronger willed, more assertive partner has probably grown up with this same feeling that led to her stronger willed position originally, the couple now really has a problem. Both are now afraid of being controlled, and both strengthen their resolve to not be controlled. They both insist on having their own way.

This difficult time in relationships is called, in the field of the psychology of relationships, the POWER STRUGGLE. When caught in the power struggle, both express strongly his or her own side of things, wanting to be understood. Since both are untrusting, and fearful of being controlled, each struggles for his own way. Usually, conflicts are resolved with one simply going ahead and doing what he wants, while the other then feels controlled, not cared for, and resolves next time to win. And the bad feelings just escalate. Both will feel they are being controlled, and both begin to lose the original love feelings.

In my thirty six years of working with couples, I have found that the best way for couples to get free from the power struggle is with an understanding of **dependence, independence, and interdependence.** Margaret Mahler, a Harvard developmental psychologist, first developed the concepts of Dependence, Independence and Interdependence in the first five years of the development of children:[9] I have

9 Margaret Mahler: Mahler, Pine and Bergman, "Two Studies", 1959 and 1963.

taken these concepts and developed a system of diagnosing and treating marital communication problems. I have found that the power struggle comes from Independence conflicts, namely, the "my way" position, together with the fear of being controlled. Independent problems grow out of the relationship with parents, and continue into adult love relationships. When an individual grows on up into interdependence, the fear of being controlled drops away, and is replaced with TRUST. The trusting feeling is based on the concept that *I care about what I want and need and value, and I care about what you want and need and value. And I believe you care about what you want and need and value, and what I want and need and value. And we care as much about the other person's needs and wants as our own.*

The way this trusting philosophy can be realized in the relationship is by understanding some simple percentages. First, each has to agree upon the idea that one can speak while the other politely listens. Each needs to get **all** of his and her inner feelings and thoughts on the difference out into the open. This open discussion of the matter is the first step. After this stage in the communication is completed, the resolution stage follows. The simple percentages come into play in the resolution stage. First, couples should always try to find a win-win resolution if it is available.

If not, one should get half of what that person originally wanted, namely to find a compromise, with the other person giving up half of what that person wanted. Only when win-win, or compromise, is not possible is it necessary to turn to win-lose solutions.

My model is that 80 percent or more of conflicts can be resolved with win-win, or compromise solutions. This leaves 20 percent or fewer to require win-lose. I encourage couples to expect the necessity of this, and therefore become more comfortable with conflict in general. Each would expect to lose 10 percent of the time, to maintain his or her love relationship. I define those times when I need to lose to my partner as an opportunity to show my caring. Knowing that my partner will know I let go of my way and allowed instead for her way, she **will feel loved and cared for because she will know I wanted the opposite**. This will increase her love in return for me. And she will be more resolved to make sure my wants and needs are met.

She will feel all the more resolved to let it go my way when another win-lose resolution is needed to resolve a difference. I teach couples to work toward the goal of **not being angry when they choose to lose, and** to conversely not feel guilty when they are given to, or win. Notice I used the words: chooses *to lose*. This is what makes this work, and takes away the fear of being controlled. In my model, I have couples agree upon the idea that one will choose to lose when the win-lose resolution is needed, rather than one going ahead with his or her own way, as happens in the power struggle stage.

When couples understand the above concept of Interdependence, and how it works - and begin to experience it - the loving resolution of differences begins to happen, and there is a snowballing of trust. Once the percentages are in mind, couples can approach each other with subjects of differences with more confidence that they can be resolved in a loving way.

Interdependence

(Author: Jan) Interdependence is the successful stage and the last stage in marital communication development. Here the couple experiences **trust.** There is no fear of being controlled. There is no stubbornness. When conflict is approached, the feelings are: I **care about what I need, want, and value, and I care about what you need, want and value. And I believe that you care about what you want, need, and value, and that you care about what I need, want, and value.** Here an individual enters conflict, freely. He expresses his own side of an issue, while his partner politely listens, and then he, in turn, listens carefully while his partner gets out her side of an issue.

Note that all dots on the figure on the next page (indicating all the feelings and thoughts inside the person, on the issue) have arrows. This means all feelings and thoughts are expressed openly to the partner. The large arrows going out the top of the circles are the empathy indicators, (namely that the person has listened carefully to the partner's feelings - even if he disagrees). In interdependence, each approaches conflict believing that his partner can see things differently, but is still equal. Each is open to being changed by this interchange, and each can **choose** to lose in order to resolve the difference, and not be angry or feel controlled. Losing is a gift to the partner, with full trust that the partner will also choose to lose another time.

When the world can do skill training for people to acquire interdependence in their relationships, whether in marriages, in parenting, in religions, in politics or in international relations, it will be one giant step for humankind.

INTERDEPENDENCE:

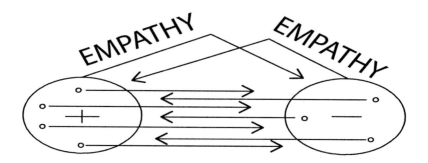

Independence

(Author: Jan) In the diagram to come the Independent stage is illustrated. In the independent stage, or power struggle, both individuals are **untrusting,** and fearful of being controlled. Both are stubborn. Both are afraid of being controlled, and therefore approach conflict with an "I cannot lose" feeling. To lose is to feel controlled. Each wants to be understood and listened to by the other. You can see there are no *empathy* arrows coming out the top of the circle. This means neither is listening to the other's feelings. They aren't open to being influenced, or changed, by the other's views. They don't take into account how the other feels. They don't seek a solution that answers the other's needs and wants. Instead of inviting differences, they fear control from the other. Therefore, they will not yield or bend. They approach the partner with their minds made up, and with a feeling that they are right. They both keep on talking at the same time. Neither wants to let the other talk.

One eventually will just go ahead and do what he wants, and when that happens, the other feels controlled, and vows to win the next time. When it goes the other way, perhaps the next time, the first person now feels controlled and not cared for. She vows to win the next time, and so the power struggle escalates. This is very painful, and you diagnose it by observing that both persons will tell you they are being controlled in the relationship. The main feeling in this stage is not trust, but feeling unloved and not cared about. The feeling is: "**You don't care about what I feel. You would gladly control me and meet your own wants and needs, and leave mine unmet.**"

Far too much of the world operates out of independence dynamics. Much of humankind's relations have been stuck here since the beginning of time. It's the way of the predator and prey. Extreme factions of the world religions still claim exclusive truth and live by "I'm right. You are wrong" and it's OK to kill you if you don't believe what I believe. Or you won't get an afterlife if you don't believe in my God. Traditional parenting functions out of, **"You will do it my way".** Still today nations largely protect their own interests instead of negotiating for each other's interests. War is the method for winning over. While democracies are founded on interdependent ideals of compromise and caring for all groups, **"my way"** politics threatens the accomplishments of democratic principles.

If a child can grow out of independence into interdependence, as healthy families help their children do, so, too, can the world evolve out of independence into interdependence. To grow out of independence into interdependence would be one giant leap for the world.

INDEPENDENCE:

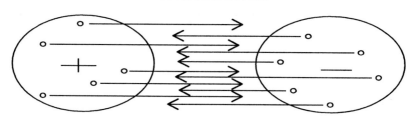

Dependence

(Author: Jan) The circle on the left in the diagram next to come illustrates a person in the dependent stage of development. Some people never grow out of this stage of development. The person illustrated here remained fixated in dependence. The person illustrated by the circle on the right was stuck in the independent stage of development. She, too, never achieved interdependence in her early child development. She is fixated in independence. The person on the left grew up keeping his feelings inside when in conflict. He automatically deferred to stronger willed family members. He developed a strong empathy capability, but was unable to self-disclose his wants and needs when in conflict with others. Hence, observe the large empathy arrow coming out the top of the left circle, and no arrows or dots from self-disclosure in conflict. The person on the right grew up with a strong ability to express her wants and needs when in conflict with others, but you'll notice no empathy arrows. She did not learn to listen to another side of the conflict. She continued stubborn and strong willed.

Many couples select each other with these patterns and then the partner on the left grows to become aware of the need to be more in charge of his life. He starts to want some say. But usually he has to go through the independent stage before he can reach interdependence. He has to win for a while to get self-esteem and feel in charge of his life. If the stronger willed partner can understand that she needs to learn how to lose without anger, she can practice developing empathy, and losing for a while to prepare herself for interdependence.

After a strong willed stage of needing to win in conflict for a while, the more passive partner can pass through independence, and move up into interdependence too. Many couples can grow through these stages, and reach interdependence once they understand where they are, and where they need to go.

Much of the world still lives in dependence and independence. Many traditional cultures, and some current churches institutionalize one sex being dominant over the other. The world still evolves towards equality.

DEPENDENCE:

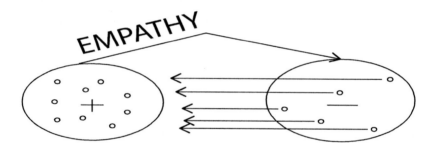

Dependent Stage Conflicts For Charles & His Marriage: And How Their Original Romantic Love Was Lost

(Author: Jan) In ideal development a person receives undivided attention in the symbiotic, or dependent, stage of development. A baby is still pretty unaware of the environment a few months after birth. She sleeps a lot, and otherwise soaks up a lot of nursing, and being held. In this way, she is reestablishing the secure feelings that were probably pretty constant in the womb. Finally, however, the baby begins to be aware of who the parenting ones around her are, and begins to enjoy an early falling in love with the parents. The smile is an indication that this stage has begun. In this stage the parents need to be very tuned in and attentive to the needs of the child for stimulation, tactility, affection, nursing and being held closely.

The child gains security, and feels loved, and is at peace with this loving attention. This can be a very enjoyable and satisfying stage for the parents too if their lives are under control enough that they can be stable, free from tension, and simply apply themselves to the child. If all goes well between the baby and the parenting ones, this stage is the building block, or foundation for all intimacy and closeness, for the child's entire life.

If on the other hand, the parents are, for whatever reason, in a crisis time in their lives, and they are stressed and distracted, it may be detrimental to the child. If the child's closeness needs are not satisfied very well, the child may become a person still in search of that closeness in later stages. However in later stages, that kind of immediate gratification is no longer possible. In later stages, when the person is now a teenager, or an adult, she still may be seeking too much attention, to be self-centered, and unable to give to others, as those stages call for.

The over use of alcohol and drugs often is an attempt to stay high and feel good all the time. Now the individual attempts to stay stoned by giving himself good feelings, when he should be facing the stresses of getting a skill, or education, in order to make money to take care of himself or raise a family.

Like a baby in the symbiotic stage, this seemingly grown up person, on the deepest level inside, wants to be cared for, given to, and taken care of, instead of taking care of others. Adults who are healthier tire of his attempt to be dependent. He wants too much attention. People around him ask him to be grown up, give and take with them, and give a lot to children and employers. The person who has not received a secure first year in life always feels: "Out to sea". He feels like he is on swirling waters, never to know the joy and challenge of being strong and giving competently to his children, his partner, and to his world. The hunger for dependence lingers, to interfere in all that he should be doing and enjoying.

Research is showing now that competent and loving parents, together with the aid of competent day care workers, and competent baby sitters, can see a baby through this stage successfully. A nervous and distracted parent, or a neglecting day care situation, can contribute to the unresolved symbiotic stage that we are considering here. If the first stage in life doesn't go well, and is not resolved right, then all the stages to come would not go well. The next stage, the separating into healthy individuality, would not go well either. And the interdependence that we considered above simply is never accomplished.

A healthy adult only needs occasional moments of fusion with the loved one, where boundaries of individuality are set aside in favor of a sense of closeness and oneness. Healthy lovemaking is obviously one measure of such connectedness. All separateness is put aside for moments where it is as if two people are one. Hugs are firm and meaningful, and each pleasures the other in a way that both are as one, in the giving and the taking.

Separateness and individuality are set aside for a while in favor of ecstatic oneness. When the lovemaking is over and the need for oneness is met, people transition very easily back to the life of each, picking up leadership, and giving to the world, each in his own spheres and dimensions. A conversation between two people can do the same thing. This is true if each is being nicely open with all his thoughts and feelings, and each is nicely listened to by the other. This intimacy is also a healthy fusion of two people into one intimate conversation.

Conflict and differences come back up as part of the warp and woof of individuality and separateness when the fusion is over. Communication of two sides or more becomes essential for the coping with reality and its demands. Standing up for one's self and one's views become necessary for working out resolutions and decisions, whether it's in a marriage, in a family, or in a democracy. All persons have to look out for themselves and interpret their needs to their partners, their children, their colleagues, and their employers. They also have to be open to the needs of others in order to meet their own needs in and around those in their environment. The dependent person continues to not do that well, but is self-centered, self-seeking, always hungry to have his needs met first and without doing the same for those around him. When women started to get together in the 1970's and talk about their experiences, some would describe the sexual experience of "slam bam thank you ma'am" where their partner would meet his own needs without regard for the partner's needs.

Besides the sexual experience example of the need for mature adults to fuse as one in mutual need, meeting moments of oneness, another recent example of the different levels of functioning was seen in the 2010 Winter Olympics. A Canadian women's figure skating competitor lost her mother from a heart attack a week before her performance. She chose to skate, as scheduled, and did a nice job of giving an aesthetic performance to the world. As soon as she finished, the tears welled up, and when she reached her female coach, the coach took her in her arms and held her for a good cry. I thought of how well this illustrated to the world the two levels of functioning, the adult performance of near perfection, followed by the regression to the symbiotic stage to collect the moment of refueling, the moment of allowing one's needs to cry and be lovingly held to regain strength. Finally, after a prolonged tight hug, the skater broke into a smile for the world to see she would be OK in spite of her enormous loss.

You will recall that Charles successfully gained sobriety from his extended alcohol and drug treatment. But you will also recall that unlike some fellow patients, Charles's defended exterior never cracked. He never broke through to be able to cry out his internal deprivation. The strong need to be held and given to never broke through, nor did the pain he carried down inside for it not having been met. If like fellow patients, Charles could have opened up to his interior pain and cried out his anger, anguish and longing to be given to, he could have benefited from the hugs of fellow patients and therapists. Hugs and holding are bountifully available once people open up to their pain. The early childhood first year emotional needs can be met in therapy. Instead, Charles remained distant and uncomfortable, even critical of that process, as people do who are unable and unwilling to go there.

Once people are comfortable with closeness and love, they are very willing to hug and hold a hurting person. It hurts to cry out deprivation pain, but it also feels good to release it, and be held by loving humans. It is such a natural and healing process. It's always a joy to watch children of all ages, even very young ones, reach out to hug and hold a crying person. Children will gladly hug and hold a parent who needs a moment of crying, and they feel very important when the parent will let them do that.

I knew of an eleven year old girl who held her father when he fell to the floor crying after hearing from his mother over the phone that his father had cancer. This man's wife, not knowing what was happening downstairs, hollered down the stairs for the girl, her daughter, to come set the table. The girl, who was cradling her father's head in her lap as she sat on the floor, hollered back up to her mother, "I can't come now Mom. I'm doing something very, very important." This example shows that letting out emotional pain, and being cared for in the moment, is a natural process that any healthy person yields to, when he needs to cry and be held. It is a universal thing. Anyone who is emotionally healthy can cry if needed, or hold those who are crying. This is an experience in giving and receiving. It is an experience of rehabilitation and healing. It is also an experience of receiving while giving, because if feels right and fulfilling for both parties.

This, of course, doesn't mean that a parent should bring all his needs for processing pain and getting support to a child. Rather, he should take those needs to his partner, or other adult friends, or a therapist. But momentary times of tearful intimacy with a child can make that child feel important. It also models to that child to be open to her own pain when such moments hit in her life, rather than turn to drugs or alcohol or other addictions, trying to cover up, bury and avoid the painful feelings.

If Charles had opened up in treatment, his future could be different than it was. Charles' unmet dependent needs continued to cause trouble in his marriage and parenting. Very early on in his adult love relationship, following treatment, Charles was in trouble. His wife began to notice that he didn't want her to live very close to her parents. In fact, her desire to be close to her parents, talk with them, and visit them often met with his disapproval. He seemed to just want all of her attention. He didn't want her to be close to anyone else. He equally resented, and tried to sabotage, any time she might want to be with friends. He was jealous of her friends and her family. He was like a baby in the first year of life. He wanted her undivided attention. His dependency needs had been unmet.

He also resented her time and attention to their children. His wife soon noticed that Charles couldn't handle all the wild emotions and loudness of children. Their children's healthy expression of wild emotions threatened to uncork his own. So he would come unglued in inappropriate ways when trying to deal with their normal fussing and fighting. Even though he had hated, and rebelled against, the harsh control and criticalness of his own parents, now as an adult, he perceived his anger toward his parents not as healthy and right, but as bad and wrong. So he turned to their philosophy of parenting, and in his wife's eyes was far too critical, controlling and punishing of his kids. He would argue that his conservative church was calling for tight control of children. He believed the return to traditional parenting was the answer to correct parenting. He would not attend psychological skill training in parenting which had been informed by scientific research.

His wife limited her own time away from home so as to protect the kids from Charles and the harsh punishment that he would carry out in her absence. She would not allow herself pastimes or hobbies as a respite from childcare, but tried to do it all herself and protect them from Charles. She tried to be a buffer for her kids. When they complained about their discomfort with him, not liking him, and not wanting to be with him, she would try to defend him to them, hoping to retain a father/child relationship. She tried to shield him from their true feelings about him, knowing he would be hurt by their pain, instead of letting him handle and listen to their pain, as a healthy parent would. A healthy parent could use children's anger and hurt emotions as feedback to look at what the parent is doing, and contemplate what he might need to correct or change to reduce their pain.

I always told my clients that love for your partner is best seen in your willingness to shoulder your half of the care for children. Being active and involved with your children not only brings you closer to your kids.

It also brings lifetime benefits to you, of your kids loving you back, and is one of the best ways to show your love for your married partner. Your partner will love you forever for your love of and caring for the children of your partnership. Parenting is a big and exhausting job, but when shared between two parents, it becomes much lighter and more fulfilling. Single parents can find someone to give them respite, perhaps a parent, a sibling, or a friend.

In a couple's relationship the partner needs to allow his spouse to be able to get away for respite. It is essential for the spouses' mental health, and very much reinforces love feelings for the partner. To be able to have friends who give you fun, energy and support helps return you to the job of parenting, renewed and happy to be with your children again. You return resolved to meet their needs well. If you are always with them and get no breaks, it's far easier to get irritable and do scapegoating that the children don't need, for their self-esteem and healthy development. To get time to have some hobbies, interests, and pastimes is also essential to your well-being. A partner who shoulders the care of children to enable his spouse to have some fun and get refreshed, will be cherished by his partner, forever and ever.

You don't need to worry about your partner losing love feelings or becoming unfaithful if you take care of her well, and meet her needs well. You will notice the good results of caring for her in the dynamic and powerful expression of sexual and love feelings throughout your years together. When underlying love needs are met, dynamic sex is the result. So is comfortable companionship. A satisfied couple is always returning to one another to talk. They look forward to returning to talk to each other, whether away for an hour, or a day, or a week.

The other area where Charles's wife was unsatisfied was when it came time to talk with him about her frustrations with the kids, work or life in general. She just never felt that talking went well. She would end up more unhappy, and unsatisfied, and lonely when their talks were over than when they began. She learned very soon that she couldn't trust him, not only with the children, but also with her feelings.

Childcare is always a demanding task, and all kinds of wild emotions and frustrations surface in a day of caring for children. You never know if you handled this or that right. What will be the result of this or that interchange? When hungry or tired children get fussy and easily turn to sibling conflict. Even though much of the day might be fulfilling and fun with the kids, there are always moments when children cry, get hurt with their siblings or playmates, and it takes patient and loving interventions to get kids through a day. When finally children are in bed for the night, a healthy home will find parents sitting down to process their days, whether from the work world or the child care world.

This is when all our own emotions come to the surface, to be gotten out and cared for, so we are renewed and refreshed emotionally to begin a new day with vigor and new optimism. Charles did all the things that have been outlined above as destructive to intimacy. His own repressed great anger and hurt was always threatening to be triggered off by his wife's pain and emotions. If she needed to express anguish or anger from difficult moments in her day, he could not be lovingly available to listen to her and accept her feelings as OK and normal.

Instead, she soon got the feeling that he believed she shouldn't be having these feelings, as if she shouldn't have bad feelings with her kids, and that she was doing something wrong. Any pain she might try to express would only trigger his strong irrational inner anger and hurt, and it would come out as criticism of her and her parenting. It was common for Charles to begin lecturing to her soon after she would try to talk. It was always about how she should be stronger in her discipline, and that she should control and punish the kids more and better than what she was doing. In other words, all the tapes of his own childhood with his parents' harsh parenting beliefs would pour out on her.

This would leave her feeling even worse than she did before they talked.

It didn't take much of this before she stopped talking to Charles about her day and turned to friends. By the time their oldest was seven years old, she had become attracted to another man and wanted out of their marriage. This, of course, was devastating to Charles, and he turned to his conservative religion, to seek Biblical text to condemn her straying eye as sinful. He continued to tell others about how she was going to burn in a lake of fire instead of reap eternal life. It's not surprising that she quit the church they had attended, and sought out less right or wrong, good and bad, devil and hell, interpretations of the *BIBLE*.

Healthy Parenting Can Prevent Independent Stage Problems: Another Giant Leap For Humankind The End Of Power Struggles In Relationships

(Author: Jan) Not only do unhappy results in marriages stem from dependency problems that come from the first year's need for closeness and meeting the baby's needs for being held, fed, and cared for on time, but problems also come from the second stage, the independent stage. After the early months of a baby's life are complete and the baby moves into the second and third year of life - often referred to as the terrible twos - more negative consequences for lifelong problems can stem from this stage, if it goes badly. The issue for a child here is that if they have felt secure from the being held, stimulated, and fed on time stage, they move more securely into the differentiating stage. Now the matter at hand is for the child to define itself as separate. She, too, has power. She can say "no." She can disagree about what she is to do next.

A child in this stage may not want to go to bed and leave her fascinating world of play and people. She may want to play instead of come to dinner, or take a bath, or a nap. Most children are kind of stubborn in this stage. This is the stage of the creative fight. A secure parent will understand the child's need for having a say sometimes. That parent works with the resistance of the child in a gentle and understanding way. The parent may suggest the nap or bedtime a few minutes early to give the child a little more time to play.

If a parent has my conflict resolution model in the back of her head, this stage of parenting can be much more tolerable. The model gives a parent a way of understanding what is going on.

It takes a lot of the worry and fear out of this stage of parenting. It's like a road map through a difficult terrain. Knowing what you are doing and where you are going keeps a person calm and relaxed instead of scared, fearful and anxious. Fear and anxiety are far too often vented through angry outbursts within family systems, and it doesn't need to be that way, if fear and anxiety are kept at a minimum.

If a parent knows she is in a healthy creative fight with her child and that the outcome will be successful, the fight becomes much less intense. My model explains that your end goal is to have a child who comes out of the fight neither too passive and dependent, nor too stubborn and defiant. In other words, you want a child who has reached the interdependence stage by the time she goes off to school. If the child gets fixated (stuck) in stage one, the dependent stage, she will have the patterns described above in my model, namely, she will acquiesce too easily, she won't stand up for herself, she won't know how to communicate her needs and wants, and she will be looking for a strong willed partner in her mate selection some day. This is the overly good child, who, in traditional parenting, looked pretty good to the parent and the community, but never really lived up to her potential, nor became a strong person in life. The reason she looked good was she was good and easy to control. She easily did what the parent wanted. The other outcome from the terrible twos that a parent won't want, the one most people fear the most, is the child that gets fixated in the rebellious response to authority. This result is that of a child who is unable to have empathy for those with whom he conflicts. He sees only his own needs and wants. He is self-centered, and selfish, to use traditional terms. He can remain stuck in the ugly power struggle throughout his life. Whenever he is in conflict, he hunkers down to win over, defeat, and have his own way, come hell or high water. This is the kind of child parents dread and fear for the teen-age years.

Unfortunately, because this result is so feared and unwanted by parents, that it is the very thing that drives many parents, and even culture as we have seen in the last fifty years, to a swing back toward strict authoritarianism in parenting. Hence we've seen the popularization of spanking again, of tight control, and support by many churches and organizations for parents to be strong authorities to their kids. It's the easiest way of parenting because most people still carry the tapes of many generations of parenting: "I'll give you something to cry about. Do it because I said so. I'm the parent, that's why. OK, no TV, no car, no friends, no dinner. You are grounded." People know how to do this simple way of parenting, and they can feel secure that they are being good parents. If their child turns out too passive, or too stubborn and rebellious, often they conclude: "There is simply something in the genes of this kid." They feel they did the right kind of parenting. Unfortunately, it's overly passive parenting, the laissez faire approach, or the overly controlling and strict approach that leads to dependent or rebellious teenagers and adults.

The overly strong willed adult that remains stuck in age two dynamics will always battle his bosses, always switch jobs due to conflict with his boss or peers, and always be prone to divorce. He'll make a strong authoritarian parent and will create some strong willed or overly passive kids. He'll always be in conflict with his strong willed kids. And he won't be particularly liked by his children.

In the model of parenting that I present here, the parent doesn't avoid conflict, nor does he rely on traditional authoritarian methods and tapes. He is a living example of interdependency. He has already mastered the communication skills to function well with the child in the terrible twos. He doesn't have to come down hard or fear his child's strong will. Here's how it works.

Most of the time when things are going right, a parent simply lives in happiness, fun, joy, and closeness with her child. It's this closeness and warmth, always, that is ultimately what a child needs while growing through all the stages. A child needs first and foremost to be liked and loved by the parent. A child needs to see the affection in a parent's face and eyes. The child needs to be secure in this love. Every day living affords most of its time up to play for a small child. If the parent can get down on the floor and play with her, she is delighted. She craves and loves the parent's companionship when the parent can be a playmate. To be a playmate, the parent needs to be a follower, not a leader. Children need to be the ones who structure their play. They can create endless scenarios and play patterns, if the parent can just follow their lead.

Stubborn and controlling adults cannot do this. They have to always be in charge of the child. They approach the child with, "Here, do this; do that; here's how you do this, why don't you try this? Here, shoot the basketball. Hold it like this. Do it like that," etc. A parent who lives in the interdependent mode can follow the child's lead in play without being threatened by it. A person stuck in independence always fears dependency, so he can't relax and let a child structure the play. A bell or whistle goes off inside his mind that he is being controlled by this child if he yields to the child's leadership. And yet what the child needs is unstructured play, where he is the one creating the situation.

Now, once a parent or grandparent can follow a child, and has the child's full attention, the parent can slip some leadership into the play, and the child can either accept it and follow a direction or if not, say so, and continue the play in another direction of his choosing. In this way skills can be taught, like how to hold the ball, etc. but it's accepted and enjoyed by the child, rather than resisted and resented.

A secure parent can allow a child some autonomy such that the child grows strong and capable. A parent who can follow in play, for example, gives the child a sense of his own power and competence, which you want a child to always retain. You want a child to come out of the creative fight, of the terrible twos, with autonomy and power intact. You want a secure and strong child to go out into the world some day.

So let's return to my model again, to see how you do this. How do you allow a child to move up into interdependence by age six or seven, instead of remaining stuck in either passive dependence, or stubborn rebellious independence?

You do it by being in the interdependent stage with children, using the skills of that stage. You always search for win-win solutions during conflict. You always use communication skills to handle the conflict, both expressing your preferences for behavior, but also encouraging them to put into words their side of it, and what they want, or don't like. If you learn to use these skills, you will be amazed how many conflicts disappear, in favor of all around good will. Just as my model described above, if you can't get a win-win solution where everyone is happy, you search for a compromise solution where each gets part of what he wants, and each gives up part of what he wants in order to get in the same ball park.

Don't you wish the "struggling to become democracies" of the world, right now, had these skills? Just like returning to traditional parenting, it seems easier to kill than compromise. It's too easy to slip back into what the world has always known: try to out-kill, win-over, your opposing group, and rule in favor of your group, ignoring the needs and wants of the losing groups. But when you look at all the results, all the death and suffering, is it really easier? One hopes it will become easier for the world's nations, and the groups within nations, to learn to compromise, and care for every group equally. If and when that happens, the world truly will take "one giant leap for humankind".

Let's return now to my model for conflicting differences within families. Most conflicts will be handled by win-win or compromise. But occasionally (I say 20 % of the time) a win-lose is necessary, and at those times you want it to go both ways. Yes, this means there are times when you choose to lose as a parent. I did this many times, and my kids are competent, capable, achieving and successful adults today. My eldest, my daughter, is a successful actuary, with a Masters in Actuarial Science. My two sons are successful men in business, both having gotten their MBAs. My kids went through their teen-age years retaining their closeness to us, liked us, and didn't get into any self-destructive rebellious groups or behaviors. That's what we all want.

We want to enjoy our kids and be close to them throughout our lives. When you hear people say that kids have to rebel, have to distance themselves from us, have to dislike us because "we have to be the heavy," you are hearing traditional parenting attitudes that lead to rebellion and distance. This is the culture's way of trying to make traditional parenting good, and keeping parents believing they are doing the best thing, when they really aren't. They are damaging their relationships with their kids, and in the really severe cases, they aren't liked at all by their children. Less severely authoritarian parents have children who do love them, yet they also feel a lot of anger and hurt, and are confused with the mix of love and discomfort they feel with their parents. The parent never knows what it's like to be loved and valued by his children, which is pretty sad. But he protects himself with traditional sayings as a way of believing he did the best thing for his kids. And without skills, and by following traditional parenting, he probably is doing the best he can. It's sad. Traditional parenting causes suffering for individuals and families, just like war causes suffering for individuals and families, and both are sad.

Yet, the art of compromise looms as "one giant leap for humankind" and the future of humankind, and the arc of history is inexorably moving toward a better future and a better world.

What is amazing to watch in the psychology of families is that kids who grew up frustrated by their parents' over-control, and rebelled and fought it, eventually turn around and decide they were bad kids for their rebellion. Now they decide their parents were right, so they set out to be the parents their parents were. They do the same kind of damage and over-control to their kids. And the rebellion, and distance, and pain, just continues down through the generations.

The parent who is in the mature stage, the interdependent stage, and has command of conflict resolution communication skills, will help his child go through the strong willed independent stage. This child will move on into interdependency by the time he goes off to kindergarten. He will be able to put himself under authority partially because he trusts and loves his parent. He will likewise trust and love the teacher. He will want to please the teacher. He will be able to follow the teacher's instructions for quietness for learning. He will be able to participate in classroom discussions because he will feel good toward the teacher. He will feel good toward his teacher because he feels good toward his parents and grandparents. He will not be filled with angry pain and stubborn resistance to authority, as are the kids who are such problems for teachers in classrooms. These are the kids who disturb the learning environment for the rest of the children.

So let's look, once again, at parenting that uses interdependent problem solving and decision making skills with a two year old. Here's how it works. We'll illustrate with some tough conflict situations. The parent can initiate some request like, "Come to lunch or time for a nap." If the child says "OK" and comes along to lunch, or goes to his nap, you have no problem. So as a parent, you can initiate for the behavior you want from the child by asking the child for a particular behavior, and the more he likes his parent, the better the chances he cooperates to please his parent. So a positive relationship is very important for handling conflict.

But let's say the parent says, "Come to lunch, or it's time for a nap" and the child resists and says, "No. I want to play more." Unlike the previous example where they came along OK, now you have a conflict situation. To use interdependent skills, you summarize the two points of view. You say: "I want you to come to lunch, or take your nap, but you want to play some more". Just to summarize the two positions is getting you out of the push-pull dynamics of traditional parenting, where you would never take time to summarize the child's request. In traditional parenting you'd simply escalate the conflict. It would be all too common to begin to threat. "OK. If you don't come to the meal, you'll get no meal, and nothing to eat till evening." Threats and power struggles come easy. "If you don't take your nap, you can't go to the party tonight" and so on.

A strong willed child will escalate with a controlling parent, even often to his own disadvantage. "I don't care. I don't want to nap". Or "I don't want to eat". Maybe the child will get angry or the parent will get angry, or both, and spanking can occur, or the punishment may start up that even the parent regrets later, when it's time for the party.

Interdependent skills might go like this: "So I want you to come to lunch, but you want to play longer, we have a problem. Can you think of any solutions?" It's far better for the child to sense that, he has some say in this, and because of that he doesn't escalate into counter power measures, or strong emotions. To ask the child to get up into his thinker is also a means of avoiding the push/pull dynamic of the power struggle. The use of these skills enables a family to stay free from turning the lunch table into an emotional battle ground. That's what you don't want.

Often in the case of lunch, there is no win-win solution unless it's a cold lunch, and if the child eats it five minutes later, or a half hour later, it doesn't really matter. But if the lunch is going to get cold, it may be one concern the parent can express, and a consequence the child may choose in order to play ten more minutes. But in that case, that's the child's choice. My kids got very good at generating solutions in conflict situations.

They would consider the two sides of a conflict as both being valid, rather than begin to see their own needs as pitted against the parents', as happens in the power struggle. But if win-win wasn't readily available, we quickly shifted to compromise. Well, the child or I would say, "How about you play for five minutes and then come? The food won't be too cold by then." I found that agreements were usually followed because the child had a say. I usually let the child brainstorm a solution and make his suggestions first. If none were forthcoming, then I'd go ahead and suggest mine.

Now if no compromise seemed to surface, a parent, in the interdependent stage, would be ready and willing to either win to solve it, or lose to solve it. Either resolution is acceptable. In losing to the child, the parent is allowing the child to learn to stay in a conflict on behalf of his needs and wants, which is a good trait for the child to carry into adulthood. Or if it's important enough, and you as the parent decide it has to go your way, the parent's way, you make that decision calmly and firmly. In this way the child is learning to yield to authority sometimes. But by going through the communications steps above, the child knows his wants and needs have been considered, but that in this case, either the parent's needs or other factors require that the child yield to the larger good.

So when the child is respected in this way, but sometimes loses, he is learning to keep himself under authority, which is so important in the classroom and in life in general. So often parents feel and believe, and some parenting programs advocate, that the child must always submit to the parent, and submit immediately. These programs take all communication out of it, as if it's manipulation on the child's part, which is never to be listened to and never allowed. I don't see it that way. I think this advice feeds the power struggle, encourages the retaining of stubbornness and rebellion, and makes either a sneaky and stubborn child, or an over-compliant child, neither of which you want.

Honesty and openness in communication, with a recognition that sometimes one or the other side simply has to yield, is a much better hedge toward the future positive development of this child. This proved to be true with my kids, and it proved to be true in my family therapy of thirty six years as a psychologist, to all ages and stages.

I have given you an example with some of the hardest conflicts between two-year-olds and their parents, namely lunchtime and bedtime. But think of it not so much in terms of one especially knotty conflict like that, but think of the repetition of this method, day in and day out, with all conflicts that come and go in the day or week with a two-year old. It's the repetition of this mutually respectful means of dealing with conflicts that leaves the child with a sense of being important and being considered in all the conflicts of his life. The child has a prevailing feeling that the parent is always considering the child's preferences and his wants. He gets a say early in his life and gets skills that will do him well when he's dealing with siblings, friends, eventually a girlfriend or boyfriend in adolescence, and ultimately in a job with an employer, and most especially in having a successful love relationship with his life partner.

Let me go back to the third solution in conflict resolution with a two-year-old. This is the solution of having it go either the parent's way or the child's way ultimately. Sometimes you, as a parent, simply have to make the decision to win and have the child yield. With a two year old, this may result in a tantrum. But when a parent knows it doesn't hurt the child to lose sometimes, and indeed, in fact, it's good for them because they are learning the important lesson of losing to others, then it's much easier for the parent. Eventually the child can lose in a more mature way. Sometimes when you as a parent use the skills correctly, you will find, much to your surprise, very often they will actually choose to lose, which everyone would believe that a two year old couldn't do. But they can, when treated this way.

But if you know that in losing they are learning to yield to authority, then you can have them yield, even if they throw a temper tantrum, and you don't feel guilty as a parent. You can explain why they need to lose this time, and proceed, not worrying if they get upset. You understand they are two years old and they are learning to yield. They learn to yield a lot sooner, I believe, because of this model. The model calls for the parent to sometimes go the way of the child when it's not the preference of the parent.

It's this kind of back and forth in the winning and losing that makes this work. The child grows out of his self-centeredness and stubbornness a whole lot sooner, when he sees that sometimes the parent is losing too, just like he has to lose sometimes. Of course, when there are matters of safety, like a child's heading toward the street, you don't stop to communicate or consider losing to the child. That's one of the times the parent calmly and firmly acts to protect the child. Because the child is young and inexperienced, it's the parent who decides when to win and when to yield.

The child comes to learn and feel the justice and fairness of the winning sometimes, and the losing to the other's preference sometimes. This skill will take the child a long ways in handling a successful adult love relationship, where each person will feel respected, but know each has to yield sometimes to his or her partner's preference. Each can do that without getting all angry or feel unfairly controlled at those times. My model is the key to successful love relationships, where two individuals feel equal and are equal.

The other patterns of submissive dependence or dominance characterize many marriages today and are the warp and woof of divorces. These patterns are the romance and love killers. It's no surprise that once no fault divorce was legal in the courts that many people chose to split up. Our children are coming out of homes where untold numbers of people are still operating out of traditional psychology, where one partner, or the other, is the dominant person. It's bred deep down in the bones of the partners' development. It's coming from the authoritarian family structure.

The founding fathers of our CONSTITUTION had achieved equality of religion and equality of the voting citizen, but the authoritarian structure of family life is still strongly supported by our culture. People need classes where the scientific method of problem solving becomes the norm in family life, rather than control and submit. Control and submit is still the watchword of large portions of the Christian church. Some of the churches flat out say that it is the man who should be the ultimate authority in the family. The argument follows literal scripture, and the male dominance of two thousand years ago. The scriptures say that if the man loves his wife, like Jesus loved the church, he will make good decisions on her behalf, and be good to her. Many churches still don't let women be on administrative boards or be clergy.

Most professionals in psychology and social work will support what I am saying in this book. But you'll find those who have followed the popular swing of culture, back to control and submit. What fascinates me about those professionals, (and they get a lot of popular press because they support traditional parenting) is that when reporters go and talk to their children, the ones they raised and lived with, you'll notice their kids don't particularly like them, and didn't like their methods of child rearing. Well, again, you'll hear "But not being a pal is good, or sure, they don't like me, but that's because I had to be the heavy." And on and on it goes.

The business world is still steaming in authoritarianism. I like the voice of Jim Collins and his book GOOD TO GREAT. In his research, he is finding that the successful CEOs are the ones who actually listen to the employees surrounding them, and invite the expression of differences. Their employee's ideas are integrated into major business decisions. His research finds that many traditional CEOs hold tight reins, only wanting obedience. These traditional CEOs think they are to tell everyone beneath them what to do. Jim Collin's research finds these kinds of CEOs aren't the really effective CEOs.[10]

He finds that big name CEOs many times are brought in to lead companies. The traditional business idea was these big name CEOs' superior thinking was to trickle down. But his data indicates they didn't do as well as did quieter, long time employees who become CEOs and listen to subordinates and care about the long-range interest of the company. It's under the leadership of these kinds of unassuming CEOs that companies become hugely successful. While Jim Collins is receiving an incredible following in the business world, he also meets resistance from the old-line business belief system. That belief system is very authoritarian. So is the American family life belief system.

---

10 Jim Collins, <u>Good to Great</u>, NY:HarperCollinsPublishers, 2001.

Examples Of Conflict In Marriage: Dependence, Independence, and Interdependence

(Dan: age fifty) As I have said before, I was very lucky in the selection of my parents and grandparents, of which, of course, I had no say at all. But I was lucky. My parents had grown up with parents who were already interdependent in their dynamics. So my parents absorbed a way of being with kids that was optimal for my development. I grew nicely through the stages of dependence, independence, and into interdependence, at least so my grandpa says.

So when I met my wife, even our dating years were smooth and largely conflict free. One difference that we had then was that my wife would rather I stopped studying earlier in the evening at college, so we could spend more time together. We talked about this more than once, and she yielded without complaining because, unlike her, I felt I needed to study in the evenings. I worked breakfasts and lunch in the dining hall, and was out for track, so there may have been some differences in our daytime study opportunities. But she was an active student as well.

I did yield some too, as I stopped studying earlier in the evenings, especially after I had established myself as a good student. This illustrates communication and compromise capability early in our relationship. We didn't blow up into angry fights over these issues, but calmly talked them out, and eventually the difference resolved, mostly through her yielding and somewhat by my compromising. She didn't get strong feelings of being controlled and chose to yield to my position. I didn't have fear of being controlled by her wanting some change. We were lucky to be free of any power struggle dynamics.

(Grandpa:) Charles and his first girlfriend illustrate the pain and trouble experienced by young couples who come from homes where their parents were fixated in dependence and independence conflicts. Charles was always passive when confronted with his father's temper and rigidity. He learned to not talk at all whenever his father would get angry with him. On the few occasions when he did try to express his side, his father turned to the traditional: "Don't talk back." If you could say there was any disagreeing with his father, it came in the form of passive behavior. Charles simply did not achieve, in any way. This was indirectly getting back at his father, in that his father, and almost all parents, wanted his child to develop well and achieve academically, and in some other ways.

It's not surprising that Charles feared conflict. In his first love relationship he avoided conflict. He simply would get morose and uncomfortable if his girlfriend would try to tell him what she didn't like. He'd try to end the discomfort by saying he would change, but stubbornly returned to the very behavior she didn't like. An example was that early on she recognized his excessive drinking. And, of course, his depression and anger began to come out when he was drinking. So their partying soon turned from getting high, to getting upset with one another.

Instead of using her feedback to move toward more moderate drinking patterns, he perceived that he was going to be controlled. So he dug in to even heavier drinking patterns. It wasn't just in the drinking area that Charles increased the very behavior she confronted, but in most every area. What was happening was that once out from under his father's thumb, Charles was trying to grow. He was moving, as people do, toward getting out of the passive dependence and become more assertive, which is a characteristic of independence. But unfortunately, without therapeutic help this young couple was thrown head on into the power struggle, the "my way, my way," dynamic.

His girlfriend had grown up in conflict with her strong willed mother. But, unlike Charles, she wasn't stuck in passive dependence. She was all out into being strong willed, and defiant of her mother. So when Charles tried to become stronger, this fanned the flames of her fears of being controlled. That's how she had felt with her mother, so she became all the more determined to not be controlled by Charles. Now she and Charles were in a nasty power struggle. Charles just continued with his drinking. They eventually went their own ways. Charles went into treatment after striking her in a drunken stupor, and she found a new love relationship.

(Dan: age sixty) As my wife and I got married, some conflicts developed. There were conflicts about where to live and how much money to spend on furniture and clothes, versus trips or a boat. There were conflicts such as what kind of vacations to take, how to handle crises of behavior with our kids, sexual frequency differences, and how to get some time with each other. There were conflicts with how to get time with friends, and how to get time for solitude and rest. All of these conflicts had to be talked out and resolved.

We recognized the need to have "work sessions". These were the times we took time and chose an appropriate place to sit down and talk. We could recognize when such sessions were needed by the fact that these differences were coming up in our daily lives and causing hurt and pain. We knew not to just burst out anytime and anywhere in these tense differing moments. We simply kept a lid on the pain and got busy setting a time and place to do the talking. It's easy to put off these work sessions in favor of simply enjoying life and wanting to be happy, and not hurt. But we trusted those sessions because we knew we would come out of them closer, and with a plan that would reduce the pain.

(Grandpa:) The procedure was that one would start describing what she wanted, and what it was that was bothering her. The receiving partner would keep his own side of it quiet, and would repeat what he was hearing his partner saying. This helped greatly to reduce the chances of escalation into "my way, my way." When one person was done expressing her side, then the second partner would begin to describe his side of it. Now the first person listened, and didn't interfere by disagreeing as soon as the other position started up.

In this way, intensity, pain and escalation into frustrated anger, was avoided. Finally, after each had spoken, with the other listening, someone would summarize the two conflicting positions, just as I said above that a good parent does when in conflict with a child. Adults, just like kids, are far more apt to see the other side of an issue when they have restated their partner's views, even when they had initially disagreed. When you repeat what the partner said, a light bulb of understanding goes off in your head. That never happens when both are talking against each other at the same time.

It's the first stage, where each describes his side of it, that painful emotions get ventilated. I say soft anger occurs at these times, because it's just part of the telling of the painful story. And when people aren't loaded with anger from their childhood conflicts with parents, they can "hear" soft anger and it doesn't create hurt or defensiveness.

When the first stage of ventilation is over for each, the love and intimate emotions begin to resurface from under the pain. Now the generating of solutions is much easier. The solutions come in the form of "win-win, or compromise," or someone "choosing to yield" and not have his way.

When these "work sessions" are over, the couple is now free of pain and tension, and new direction takes place. The couple is reconnected emotionally, and wonderful powerful love making returns to its rightful and natural place.

In each of Charles' revolving relationships similar conflicts would not resolve. In his first relationship he mostly got morose and withdrew with conflict. Gradually he started to grow and moved into independence.

Each time he and his wife would start to fight in some inappropriate situation, both would angrily blame the other in an ever escalating and painful showdown. The power struggle, with its characteristic unending fighting, would just go on and on. Never resolving differences would erode the original love that they had upon meeting and courting. Eventually each could not stand the tension and growing distance. Sexual enjoyment would gradually dry up in favor of distance and discomfort, and his relationships would eventually end in disappointing separation and divorce.

Mid-Life Success or Failure?

(Author: Jan) The payoff of healthy relationships and healthy parenting is the pride and joy of seeing grandkids well treated. The payoff is also in seeing your own adult children happy with their mate selection, and grandkids who are growing psychologically happy and well.

In this stage there is a realization of what the two of you have accomplished in the rearing of a family. If both have been active with the kids, each in turn appreciates the help each has received with the kids. Each realizes how important the other individual's role was in doing well by the kids. The love a couple has had from the beginning only grows deeper and purer in the mid years. Such a deep appreciation is felt for the role of the partner.

It's as if love refines and becomes more mellow and constant. Humor and fun bubble up between two people who have successfully met the parenting demands in the earlier years. Companionship is full of joy. You can read it on the faces of successful couples in their mid and later years. They are fun to be around. There is a glow that nourishes everyone they see.

On the other hand, if one parent wasn't very involved with the children, this reality will remain as a thorn between the partners. One feels guilty that he didn't do enough and the other feels resentful that her partner left the load up to her. Partners in this circumstance can never be as fulfilled, appreciative and purely loving as the couple who each carried his fair share. Partners, who observe their own dysfunctional patterns being played out by the next two or three generations, cannot be as content, fulfilled and satisfied in their middle and older years.

On some deep level they know there had been patterns out of control within themselves that they never took the time and effort to discover, study, get in control of, and stop. Many times these persons turn to ancient religious concepts for comfort. They seek to believe that human inadequacy and fallibility are built into the fabric of nature, and that a cosmic request for forgiveness for sin which they couldn't control is answered by a pure and strong love for them, regardless of what they have done. Often this view is the only way they can find peace and consolation.

But now, with modern psychology, we have the knowledge and skills to stop pathology and free children and grandchildren from going through the suffering and pain their forefathers and foremothers suffered. Unfortunately, this scientific knowledge has not become dominant in the realities of marriage and parenting. Long revered and cherished philosophies of pathology and human suffering still hold sway in large value pools.

What I mean by this is that some of these communities with shared values have mistaken self-love and assertiveness in children as selfishness and rudeness. Some traditional communities within Christianity turn to St. Paul, who said, "We shouldn't think too highly of ourselves." Children and adults who are arrogant or condescending are those who are covering up great internal emotional pain. Arrogance is a defense against bad feelings inside. People with repressed bad feelings pass them on to others, making others feel bad.

Children raised with psychologically skilled parenting are comfortable to be around. They are not critical or defensive. They don't think too highly of themselves. But they are confident, and internally secure. They are self-accepting and self-loving. They are relaxed and respectful of other people. They are affectionate, open to feelings, and can be warm to others. They make friends easily and can have fun.

The war between new healthier ways to treat kids and the old ways still too often tilts in favor of the ancient and psychologically uninformed. I live in a university town that abounds in bright, specialized, and highly educated persons who don't realize how little they know when it comes to psychological skills of listening, respecting and affirming people around them. As a therapist in this town for thirty three years, I know the struggles, and the problems of some of the professor's children and grandchildren.

In their elder years, many of these highly educated people know that their children and grandchildren are not growing up very happy, content and fulfilled. They kind of know that they themselves were a part of that same sad drama, but don't quite know how. In their later years they strive for some modicum of stability and peace of mind by turning to religion, or distractions, or travel.

I've seen them sometimes condemn their children and grandchildren for going through the same problems they went through. It's as if their kids and grandkids should know how to avoid the problems, when they themselves didn't know how to avoid them. It's an on-going saga of human suffering. It results in divorces, child custody battles, drug and alcohol problems, various forms of abuse in relationships, and medical problems. As a therapist in a university town, I know the painful power struggles that have gone on in academic departments and the administrations, not only of the university, but schools, and churches, and businesses. Improved parenting could produce fewer people prone to power struggle dynamics. All of society's institutions could benefit from people's learning how to become interdependent.

On the other hand, the university towns have many people who have benefitted from the healthier ways that many university departments are giving to their students and to society at large. The extension services at Iowa State University are making available the insights of the healthy revolution my book expresses. The culture of the midwest has been very positively impacted in the last fifty years and is showing great improvements in psychological health and well-being. The arc of history will continue in this new positive direction. Skill training in schools could much enhance the health of a country.

The university towns also abound in people who are paving the way for the healthier revolution that my book is about. Amongst all the excellent research and education of the great universities is the research and education towards the better psychological health of society. For instance, Harvard's largest attended class ever is a class in positive psychology. Students are highly motivated to improve their chances at a happy and fulfilling life.

Many universities are starting classes in positive psychology. Dr. Emma Seppala is Director of Stanford University's Center for Compassion Research and Education. She has a class on happiness and well-being. Dr. Christopher Peterson has a similar program at the University of Michigan. Dr. Martin E.P. Seligman has done similar work at the Universities of Pennsylvania and Princeton.

In the late 1990s, as Chairman of the American Psychological Association, Dr. Seligman announced that the APA needed to add positive psychology for the happiness of normal people to its traditional mission of curing abnormal psychology problems for mentally ill people. The arc of history will continue in this new positive direction. Inexpensive and available skill training will soon be possible for the masses through the internet. Due to modern communication, a new day is dawning for people throughout the world to become healthier through psychological education.

There are some thriving programs available in couple communication skill training. MindTools.com has a good program with listening skills and communication skill training. John Gottman has a program for couple conflict resolution available at www.happycouplesacademy.

An excellent parent education group very close to the skills of this book is available at www.activeparenting.com. And the American Psychological Association has both positive parenting skill training and advanced training for professionals to run parenting workshops at www.apa.org.

If Charles' parents had access to skill training like this, Charles' life could have been different. Dan's life illustrates how well a life can go in all stages if parents and grandparents have had human relations skill training. The morning news would not have to be so full of tragedy, incarcerations, spousal abuse, and murder if society would make available the skills scientific psychology already has accomplished.

Mid-Life Contrasted To Earlier Stages

(Grandpa:) In contrast to all the suffering that I've described, in a highly educated demographic, people who have had the good fortune to grow in relationship skills can have a much better mid-life experience. When all the previous stages of life have gone well, this stage is where "life begins." The kids will be getting on into college, the military or the work world. Partners can, for the first time, get more time with and for each other. They can have more time for themselves. Finally their days and evenings can be for doing as they please. It's a wonderful time in life. Mid-life is also usually the time for the dying of parents, while on the other hand, receiving new grandkids into couples' lives.

(Dan: age sixty three) Helping my parents in their elder stages was a positive time. The effort and work that it brought to take care of my parents' homes, and to move them into retirement centers and nursing homes was far made up for by the opportunity it afforded for closeness to my parents. Prior to this, I was busy with career and raising kids. Now the kids were out of the home. I was retired, so I could devote my time to being with my terminally ill parents. Now I could reestablish the close bonds of my original years with my parents.

This time I was seeing to their needs and looking out for them. Time was now available for long and enjoyable conversations. They shared memories of the past. They discussed the business with which they needed help. We shared about past and present events of our family. Our relationship had come full circle. It was a very enjoyable stage for both my parents and for me.

(Grandpa:) For Dan's parents, the warmth of this relationship with Dan tempered the challenges of terminal illness and facing death. It made all the difference in the world to them. He told them it was a precious opportunity for him. Nothing excels positive human love when it goes right.

For Dan mid-life was also a time where he found he needed to rest more. Intense family gathering days, or outside work on the property, all of a sudden needed to be followed by some quiet resting days, as the energy was no longer boundless. Intense days or evenings out with friends required quiet resting days at home the next day due to this new discovery that intensity has to be made up for by rest and recovery. This may be a sign that mid-life is beginning to give way to the needs of the young-old stage that begins in the late sixties and early seventies.

If consideration is given to this new ebb and flow of energy, and welcomed, it can be a time of reflection. There finally is time for remembering all that has gone on before. Wonderful memories of his children growing up accompanied wonderful memories of his own childhood years. A sense of satisfaction took place for Dan that the previous stages were done right and well. He enjoyed a peaceful glow in his periods of rest and restoration. A slowing down to contemplate, remember, and enjoy is the pay-off for a life well-lived up to that time.

Some people are afraid of slowing down. They see it as weakness or unwanted aging and inadvertently rush on by.

The love for grandkids became the new joy of this stage for Dan. An enjoyment of their development was at the heart of this stage and later. For Dan a sense of satisfaction took place because he had done the parenting right and well. The grandkids and their positive development was his reward. Dan cleared his schedule to have regular and prolonged time with his grandkids. He got on their level, just as he had done with his own kids. And they loved him for it. And he loved them deeply. He enjoyed them immensely.

For Charles, the opposite happened. Charles never reconciled with his parents. He couldn't stand to be around them, and they couldn't stand to be around him. Great resentment came between them that went both ways. Charles stayed away as much as possible. His parents were without the closeness and protection that only adult children can bring the elderly. Their lives became increasingly lonely. They weren't any better at getting close to friends than they were at parenting.

In Charles parents' attempts to make friends in their adult years, Charles' father would invariably offend people. When attempting social occasions, people would become hurt by his father's way of putting people down. His father was bossy and offensive. Any efforts at planning joint activities, like travel with others, would result in people not asking to repeat the experience. He had to be in control, and didn't have the ability to give and take that joint travel requires. So not only were Charles' parents without the protection of adult children's support, but they were also without friends. They were alone to face the trials of aging, terminal illness, and death.

Besides the distance and unresolved pain of alienation from parents, Charles also watched the painful results of what he didn't do right with his kids. Now it was affecting a whole new generation of people who were trying to grow into their teenage and adult lives. The "chickens came home to roost." And what made it worse is that he didn't know that he was the cause of it all. His church gave him the answer, that his grandkids like himself were sinners. This helped him feel better. He didn't know he could have been responsible for how he had parented.

But his parents' pathologies, and his own response to chemical dependency treatment, did not result in his stepping up to the requirements of self-discovery and self-exploration. He never got free of the bad feelings of his childhood.

He wasn't up to the task of opening up to heal. It remains true that people are responsible for how they parent and live the stages of their lives, regardless of whatever pathologies their parents passed on. If people inherit psychological problems from inadequate grand parenting and parenting, and do not take advantage of modern psychology to learn better and do better by their kids, the kids will continue the downward spiral of dissatisfaction, dysfunctional relationships, and unfulfilled mid-life.

Healthy Growth Results In Religious Responses Of Gratitude And Wonder: Dan Shares A Moment Of Peace And Love

(Dan: age sixty-five) Evening has come. My little grandson is a delight. He loves me so. And I love him so.

This week he played on our driveway in the setting sun while I sat on a lawn chair and admired his every move. He worked hard in his play. Moving the fire truck off the drive into the grass, over a bit of a drop, seemed to intrigue him the most.

Oh Lord God, what is man that thou art mindful of him? This is Judaic Christian biblical poetry with the built-in belief that God is mindful of us. Perhaps we say that because there is an inner need for it. Maybe life is so insecure, or so beautiful, that we need a God for solace and hope of safety. Maybe we need a God to explain our response to beauty and gratitude. When things go right, we can feel so grateful for our lives, for beauty, for fun, for joy and pleasure. Maybe we want to thank someone or something bigger than just what is here.

If our parents were good at parenting, we will want to thank them. If they were good at parenting, then they truly gave us a lot. But still people generally seem to be glad to grow up and be free of daily living with their parents and family of origin. It seems people want to be free in the world. It appears that people want to manage their own lives. They want to be in charge of themselves.

Yet, if life goes well, it seems we want to express gratitude and thankfulness to something bigger. Our parents met our early needs and then we took over, but we may feel we never stand alone in the world. If we feel we are here with love all around us, it may give us a feeling that there is a larger plan, by some bigger loving being. It's a feeling that this wonderful life must be a gift. Most world religions postulate that there is a universal love that is the source.

When earthly love relationships are so totally fulfilling, it seems logical that they may be an extension of a transcendent source of love. Our family and friends give us courage to move on toward life's end. Since we are accustomed to wonderful love relationships, it makes sense that a greater love would be waiting for us beyond this earthly existence. It's just too good to stop. Love seems so strong.

I enjoy bonds to people on this earth that never seem to fade. If I knew them well at some point in my life I always will know them. My relationships with those people remain fresh and alive and full of love and joy, even if I haven't seen them for years and years. If we get to meet sometime, the feelings have not changed. Love just doesn't seem to fade. Other things change and fade. But love doesn't seem to. When life goes well and you've loved many people it's easy to conclude that surely love continues on the other side of death. Life seems to be about love.

(Grandpa:) But maybe beyond all these needs that a faith in something bigger meets, maybe a zest for life springs out of that same larger-than-life being. Maybe our love of life springs from it. Nothing is better than the driving inner lust for life. A baby longs to crawl, though crawling is difficult to figure out when the baby is eight months.

A crawling baby longs to get up and walk, and when she first does it, she is thrilled. A five year old longs to go to school and when he does it he loves it (unless some pathology stands in the way). The elementary child longs to enter middle school. The middle school graduate longs for high school. The high school graduate longs to get off into the work world or college and to be independent from home.

The college graduate longs for life. The feeling is "let me at it". Young people love to travel. They have parties, and climb mountains. They enjoy their freedom and they love to "hang out" with friends just as we seventy four year olds do. Young couples, after a period of freedom, long to have a baby, and in spite of the hardships of it, they are proud and protect their fledgling. They feed it faithfully, and have another as soon as they can. Most young adults want a family.

Some couples can't have their own children. And some couples make a conscious decision not to have children. They can benefit from freer lives. They can have more time for each other and more money for their interests, hobbies and travel. And the skills of this book can be equally useful for them in their own relationship, and in their vocations. Many times they love nephews and nieces and can use these skills to nurture their extended family ties.

Life seems to demand the next stage, always. And with each new stage people go for it with zest. There is a zest for living. We are about life's tasks and challenges with a vehemence. What gives us this drive? Does nature alone do this? Or is there something built into nature that drives life forward with such excitement, mastery, and love of mastery?

Maybe there's a life force, a joy in living, a living with exuberance that brings a hypothesis of God into being to explain such mindful mastery. Usually people aren't sitting around worrying about death.

Our minds are made, it seems, to concentrate. Our fingers are to do things. Our focus brings joy, the joy of simply living and doing. Our built-in abilities are made to be used, just as my restored tractor almost seems to enjoy working, rather than just sitting around for show. It's made to work. We are born to use our inner skills. I can sit contentedly for hours and write. I have no idea where the ideas are coming from, and I don't know what's going to come up next but I love watching the ideas appear on paper.

(Dan: age sixty six) Today I'm close to that depth. I'm rooting myself in it. I'm calling for its love of me. When I pause and wait patiently and be still, a feeling of deep connection to it takes place. There is a moment of security. The moment also includes an "accepting of the great universal acceptance." I have a sense of being loved ultimately. It hurts, it feels so good. It is a deep awareness of that which is usually subconscious, beneath life's hurrying and scurrying.

In the presence of this gratitude, this feeling of being loved, this pure acceptance of love, all of a sudden my individuality doesn't seem so terribly important. As a part of this bigger thing, I can now let death come without regret or worry. I can let go, just as I let myself be born into awareness at one time, seventy four years ago. At that time, I knew nothing about what was ahead. I didn't know loving arms would be there to receive me. But they were. And this world is real. Why couldn't it happen again?

Healthy Religion Versus Unhealthy Religion: Healthy Countries Versus Unhealthy Countries: The World In Need Of Another Giant Leap

(Author: Jan) Dan has described a religious experience, his religious moment. He demonstrates how his faith brings him great moments, and brings him comfort and trust, as he gets older and must get comfortable with his own immortality. We can have our own healthy religious response, even in a time when the world religions seem to get entangled with man's pride, fears, aggressions and hates. I can still embrace my individual religious response, even while observing the craziness and sickness of the competition of the world religions. Another wish I have for humanity is that one day all children everywhere could receive an education that presented the beginnings of world religions as a stage in developmental history.

If the human being on earth could learn all the religions together at once, a new world citizen could be born. This citizen could see the merits of all religions, as they were born in a stage of history when man was first beginning to formulate a religious response to our lives on earth. Now, far too often it seems people grow up exposed to the teachings of one religion, as if it were the only one. Competition and hate for other religions is the result of this localization of viewpoint. People start to want to hate that which isn't familiar to them. They want to put their own religion over and against all others. So many wars have been the result.

Instead of peace, love and harmony with their fellow humans, it brings out the worst in human beings.

The great Harvard psychologist William James in 1902 published The Varieties of Religious Experience.[11] He studied the religious experience in many parts of the world. He found that the content of people's religious experience always matched the symbols, images, and morality of whatever particular religious community that individual was shaped by. None-the-less, religious experiences the world over were viewed by individuals in divergent cultures as of ultimate value. If William James' research was known across the world, people could learn early on that God might come to people through many different leaders, with many different ideas of God and culture. People would be far less likely to grow into competition against, and hate for, other religions. There will be a new tolerance for divergent cultures when the psychology of religious experience is better understood by all people throughout the world.

John Hick was a philosopher and theologian from Oxford, England, who has worked hard to encourage religions all over the world to see how much they have in common. John Hick died a few years ago. I hope someone picks up his mission. He urged the world religions to identify those ideas that lead to separation and hate, and challenged them to question these destructive beliefs.[12]

Many religious leaders the world over listened to John Hick. I believe the arc of history will go in the direction Dr. Hick has brought to the theological and philosophical world. As this view spreads, religionists the world over will need to examine their own "my way" view of things, and realize how much pain and suffering it has brought to the world, in its development, and in its current conflicts. Extreme groups of the world religions today use their Holy Scripture to justify killing their opponents.

There is a wise saying: "This too will pass". It seems to me much of the world is growing weary of the hate and killing from such extreme groups. So much of the world's historical religious

---

11 William James. The Varieties of Religious Experience: A Study in Human Nature. NY: Longmans, Green & Co. 1902.

12 John Hick. "A Pluralist View." "More than One Way? Four Views on Salvation in a Pluralistic World". Eds. Dennis L. Okholm and Timothy R. Phillips. Grand Rapids, MI. Zondervan Publishing House, 1995.

thinking has been of the stubborn, "my way" stage of development. Horrifying beliefs of tortured afterlives, have been used to scare and manipulate people to adopt a given faith community. Much of the religious world is evolving past such primitive thinking. Renowned historian/sociologist Marvin Harris says that religions that were rooted in some "holy script" had better chances of surviving than those that wrote nothing down.[13]

It was easier to convince people that the religion that had writing was more valid. Individuals who had religious experiences, whose followers would listen to them and write what they said down, would testify to whoever might listen. Religions appear to have begun in very much authoritarian ways. The inspired leader spoke from a "this is the way it is" point of view. In these early stages, thinking yourself was probably not understood. The preacher's pulpit to this day is largely used to sway people in the way of the preacher's views. The biblical phrase that encourages "Thy way, not my way" is rooted in a belief system that we should seek for God's will, not our own, as if our own thinking would always be sinful and wrong. A lot of our faith and worship is still based on pre-democratic terminology.

Much of the Christian church and probably most world religions are still rooted in an authoritarian model. Although many churches today encourage the development of the individual's own faith. These churches encourage people to respond to sermons, and that it's OK not to agree. Tolerance of different viewpoints is growing. This is a good trend toward respecting the individual's ownership of her own faith.

Preaching to convince is a long established means of attempting to sway others to adopt a view point that is held by the speaker's group. Too often, anyone who questioned or disagreed was viewed as bad in some way, much like a child whose behavior the traditional parent would like to extinguish.

The importance of people having the right to think for themselves and to choose their own theology and values has emerged in the recent growth of democratic philosophies.

13 Marvin Harris. NY: <u>Our Kind.</u> NY: Harper & Row. Publishers. Inc. 1989.

When modern scientific psychology came along in the last two hundred years, it, too, found that individual freedom to choose a faith was a much healthier way for people to live. Democracy has adopted this idea. Now can religions catch up? Just as modern families must become more democratic, religions must become more democratic. Flexibility of beliefs and openness to value differences can make religions much healthier and much less warlike.

In recent history many parents have learned to tolerate theological and value differences from their children. Family life for many families has become so much more harmonious than when parents attempted, throughout history, to control the theology and values of their children. Families who have evolved in this way no longer reject or kick their children out when they disagree about values or theology. They can love one another and stay together, even if they do differ. They can be at peace.

Inner racial, inner faith, inner denominational marriages could now take place, instead of family wars and rejections. Human relations have taken one giant psychological leap forward. But that leap is still in its infancy. Large pools of faith communities still insist on their own way and acceptance is based on doctrine or belief. Pressure is brought to bear. Children are sheltered from the values of the world as older generations attempt to control the environments and beliefs of their children. Indoctrination versus freedom to believe still holds sway, far more than what is good for the world to heal and to get along.

There is still a long way to go before the "lion lays down with the lamb". Stubborn "my way" thinking is still huge and rampant in the world. But the arc of history is moving inexorably toward a healthier tomorrow. The psychological discovery of the "Interdependence" is one giant leap for humankind. Mature people who can discuss varying religious or value differences without escalating into anger, coercion, and rejection are a breath of fresh air to the world. Humans have battled to the death over minor doctrinal differences. All of a sudden that looks so ridiculous and so sad. More and more, these fanatical and dogmatic religious views will be released in favor of cooperation and love. Caring about one another is so much better than caring about me, and mine, while attempting to use and reject you, and yours.

Marvin Harris says many of the world's original societies would eat the losers of war for protein. Later in man's development, when empires could produce much more food due to specialization and agriculture, and protein wasn't so scarce, the losers of war became slaves who could contribute to the winner's wealth. Losers of war could be used for the benefit of the winner, rather than eaten.[14]

The next step now is to actually care for others, as well as to care for ourselves and our own. This is new. Caring for oneself and one's own, and competing for resources with others, and killing them rather than caring about them too, was the way of the world. And, of course, you still see it in the world today. Societies have evolved to "my way – my way" and dictatorships and war are the mechanisms to keep the world fixated in this stage.

People who want to keep this view and justify it, say, "But look at the animal world. That's the way it operates. We are animals. We can't help it. That's the way we are". Yes, but we humans, with our advanced brains, can take the next step and rise above our animal natures. We have even begun to care about animals and the eco systems of the planet, rather than just care about ourselves. The two Roosevelt presidents fought hard against special economic interests to save national monuments, our forests, and our most beautiful national parks, for the entire public to enjoy, instead of just the rich and powerful. Interdependence - instead of the "my way" - holds for a much better future world.

That would be a world that cares about everybody. People can learn to care about me and to care about you, too. The nation states generally follow the rules that convey: "I will protect my interests and you protect your interests." This means

14 Martin Buber. I Thou. London: T & T Clark, Ltd., 1937.

we are fixated at the Independent stage of development. To reach Interdependence in the future, we will live by: "You and I protect my interests, and you and I protect your interests." The arc of history is moving in that direction. Moral humans will get there, because moral humans will succeed over immoral, or amoral, humans." Life evolves slowly.

It is so much fun to get to know persons from other cultures, and to let them into our lives to share and care. The new skill of being able to talk about theological or value differences opens up such a nice world of brotherly love. And history has many examples of when cultures get to know each other well, they fuse and eventually become one. Becoming more like one another is so much better than stubbornly trying to win over each other by mechanism of war. Trust and safety are so much better than fear and violence. Let's return to Dan and his expression of how a faith works for him.

(Dan: age sixty eight) I don't push my individual faith on anyone else. But for me, I do seem to need a personal faith. It's a faith of wonder, trust in life and death, appreciation, and great love.

If life doesn't go well, like for Charles, religion may be a desperate hope for a better life ahead. My old friend Charles might say something like this: "I'll stick with the old time religion. I need salvation from my past behavior. I'm a sinner. I need a God to take over my sorry life. I hope for a better afterlife than this veil of tears. God please forgive me, for I have sinned. I'm alone in this world. I'm on my own to face death. Please be there for me."

(Author: Jan) I look forward to a future where skill training that protects the natural love feelings can be universal. Martin Buber was a theologian in the early twentieth century who recognized that something seemingly magical happens within relationships. He spent some time observing psychiatrists being trained. I, too, was in a training program where Harvard psychiatrists received daily case conferences from outstanding experienced teaching psychiatrists. I witnessed daily the power of human relationships to heal the mentally ill.

By the time the theologian Martin Buber wrote I THOU, psychology was beginning to understand how skills could protect the love feelings in relationships. He believed that God's original source of love was communicated through human love. All human love, he postulated, pointed to and was an expression of the loving power of the creator. He saw that human dialogue was the source of security and comfort in this world. **** A contemporary theologian of Buber, Harvard theologian Paul Tillich made society aware that people had a courage and vigor that defied the existential anxieties of living. He felt that vigor and courage was evidence of an ultimate source of love. He, like Buber, thought that love overcame the fears of living and dying.[15]

Some churches lift up the requirement that you accept Jesus as your savior so that you inherit Eternal Life as if everything else would then go well for you. But, like Charles, you still may not know how to raise your kids in a way that they can love successfully and well. Wouldn't it be wise to follow up religious conversion experiences with relationship skill training that actually meets people's needs to feel loved, and enhances their capacity to love? It may not be enough to be converted to a belief in Jesus and then be told to "go and sin no more". Today we know how to teach people to love successfully. People who love successfully don't go harming other people. If you wish to avoid sin, teach people how they can be deeply happy and satisfied in powerfully loving relationships. If God is love, and is an enormously powerful supreme being who created the world and wants humankind to love one another, let's train humans to love successfully, now that we know how to do that. I don't think God was revealed only through the Holy Scriptures of world religions alone. If God is revealing himself as love I think he continues to reveal himself. And if so, I think he has revealed himself through scientific psychology. To know how to love successfully is one giant leap for humankind. Science and religion can cooperate instead of compete.

15 Paul Tillich. The Courage To Be. New Haven: Yale University Press. 1952.

I have a loved one who survived a forty eight hour fire fight in Iraq. Many of his buddies did not survive. He followed my guidance to join a Veteran support group and has added individual therapy. He is handling his terrible trauma quite well six years later. Can worship services, prayer and faith in God alone heal severe human trauma without these face to face talking therapies? I don't think so. If God heals then God's healing is in the talking therapies. Most religions believe God is love. When people can love by being open with one another, hurt together, provide human affection while the pain is released, it would be logical that God is there. If God is love, then loving well is expressing God.

(Author: Jan) Self-centeredness comes from the developmental flaws when children's needs are not met accurately and adequately. Psychopaths and other personality disorders come from deficient and uninformed parenting, not simply that they are in the grips of the devil. Many churches strive to bring religion to psychopaths through their prison ministry (which is admirable and caring). The message is that if they accept God's love of them, they can reform and start a good life. They are forgiven. Some do stop their criminal behavior with enough loving attention from the church. But let's not create psychopaths to begin with. Let's stop it where it starts – in the home. We need more than remedial work after great harm and violence to others has taken place. Let's prevent it. Relationship and parenting skill training are sorely needed. We have the knowledge. Now we need to train people to be good partners and good parents.

My skill training model for Interdependence applies to countries too. Descartes, Locke, and Hume followed early Greek thinking about representative democracy. The idea was that power and authority should not be the rights of individuals who were born into a royal family, or individuals who were the leaders of the most powerful farms or clans.

Instead of changing leadership through war from disgruntled opponents, leadership would change through election where the majority of the people gave power to leaders. Beyond that, the losing minorities' interests and needs were to be taken into account through compromise of the people's representatives.

The United States has made democracy work. For it to work, people had to agree to compromise, and the minority who did not win an election had to be willing to be governed by the majority's choice. My relationship model calls for seeking consensus first. If that's not possible, seek compromise – each giving up something to meet in the middle. If that doesn't work, one side chooses to lose. In the United States, when one party loses to the other, the culture of democracy calls for the losing party to gracefully accept the loss and put itself under the leadership of the winning party.

Iraq is trying to become a democracy now, but democratic candidates are at risk of being shot by the opposing factions. This is the way the world has always operated. It's MY WAY. It's I CARE ABOUT ME AND MINE, BUT NOT YOU AND YOURS. The United States has been a model of how democracy no longer has to have violence in order to change leadership. Society has to achieve interdependence in order to do this. Today we are in a crisis as to whether we can continue to advance democracy, or revert into factions that hate one another and will no longer agree to lose to the other in the democratic way.

The drive to win over, try to control, and not follow the opposing party's leadership appears to be gaining sway. We are at risk today of slipping back to the independence ways of the past, the MY WAY that is paranoid about being controlled, and believes the other side won't care, and wishes to win over the other side. Our political factions are losing TRUST of the other sides, and losing caring for the other side. Hopefully, we can see our way through this difficult time in history.

Interdependent skill training in families would create far more citizens who trust and understand how democracy works, and create fewer authoritarian personalities. People who live by control or be controlled dynamics don't make good representatives of the common good. We have lots of business people who care about their employees and the common good as well as their profits, but we still have some who will put their own profits ahead of the good of their employees and of the common good of the country at large. Skill training of families would help develop business people and congressmen who care about everyone equally.

Mid-Life: A Time When Marriage Can Sail To New Heights

(Author: Jan) Mid-life is a time when marriage can sail to new heights if previous stages of marital development were healthy. When a couple has reached financial security, and can let go of their work identities, time is now available for fulfillment in their relationship. Prior to this time in life other responsibilities must come first, namely work and children.

Finally the pace can slow to a level that offers the opportunity to maximize love relationship potential. Now each individual works toward a new identity that can result in interesting conversations with one another. The task of this stage is for each to use time to find his true identity, the identity that is beyond parenting or career identity. For very possibly the first time in life, they can use time to seek out activities or involvements that interests them purely for the interest alone.

In mid-life and retirement, people may lose their work identities and co-worker connectedness in favor of new pastimes and new relationships. Their marital partner is the one they come home to, and process whatever activities and new friendships they are discovering, with the new time and space in their lives. These changes require and foster the couple's own intimate conversations, where excitement, interest, and sometimes the challenges are expressed to one another.

When healthy, young couples fall in love and commit to each other. After that, they spend considerable time talking with each other about their growing adult identities and activities. The same is true for newly retired couples. They, too, will spend considerable time talking about their identities and activities. They provide each other with support, comfort and encouragement.

Only this time the conversations don't have to wait until the work day is over and the kids are listened to and supported before their bedtimes. Now a spouse can come home mid-morning from an art class and sit down over coffee with his partner, to share his new discoveries.

There is a new flexibility to catch opportunities to share and be together. The longings, yearnings and necessary deprivations of earlier stages of a marital relationship can more easily give over to better fulfillment of intimacy needs. If a retired couple wants to make love in the morning and rest a while before starting their day, they can do that, if they are careful to keep a schedule that isn't too packed with obligations to others. The key to closer marital bonds and greater marital fulfillment is the ability to slow the pace and make time for each other.

I Have A Dream Too

(Author: Jan) It would be a nice leap for humankind if the vast majority of couples could reach a fulfilling stage of marriage in their senior years. Eight years after Martin Luther King Jr. left the Boston University School of Theology, I arrived for my seminary education there. His dream is well documented in the hearts and minds of people all over the world. I have a dream that one day couples throughout the world could reach and enjoy this stage of life in a happy and fulfilled way. I love John Lennon's words about imagining all the people living life in peace.

I hear Lennon's song when I let myself dream of the future. Skills are available now to realize this dream for the world, but again, it will be generations before this kind of emotional and relationship training will find its way out to the peoples of every country on the planet. But it will happen. And it's very touching to picture. I spent twenty of my career years as a psychologist doing couple communication skill training. My wife and I would travel to some spot in the three county catchment area that the Mental Health Center served, and do skill training seminars. To keep our role plays lively and fresh, we'd struggle to dig up some area in our relationship where some irritating unresolved difference might still be plaguing us, mild though it were. If a couple has conflict resolution capability early in their marriage, it really isn't very long before any potentially big differences are put behind them. After that, they are blessed with conflict free companionship most of the time. But as life brings growth and changes along the way, invariably new differences will surface to also be resolved. By the senior years, successful couples can be amazingly free of conflict.

Since my wife and I were good at conflict resolution due to our having been lucky to choose professions that gave us precious training, our relationship continued smooth, loving and very fulfilling. So it wasn't always easy to find small, irritating unresolved issues for our seminars. But interestingly enough we always came up with something. And since these were weekly Wednesday night workshops for six weeks, we had a nice means to keep on top of our issues. Otherwise in busy family and work schedules, it can be difficult to find time to trace down conflicts and work on them. And there's nothing like fresh, live unresolved couple material to keep workshop attendees on the edge of their seats.

We would take up an unresolved issue between us and use the skills to demonstrate to people how to handle differences in a constructive and creative way. We'd work till we had a solution. Then we'd turn back around and demonstrate traditional destructive conflict communication on the same exact issue to show people what that all-too-familiar scene looked like. While the constructive conflict skills were usually unheard of by the participants, the destructive communication role modeling brought moans of familiarity. We would work the issue with dependent/independent dynamics. Then we'd work the issue with the "my way – my way" power struggle, independent/independent dynamics. After that, couples in our workshops would have time to practice the positive skills on current issues of their own. My wife and I would circle the group to coach their work. If the future can find a way, and it will, skill training like this in religious groups, schools, colleges, and businesses can bring about a new and better day.

To this day, now at seventy four years of age, my wife and I have had many, many years of satisfaction seeing so many of our seminar couples still happily together after all these years. We like seats that are high in the Iowa State University Basketball Coliseum to escape bright lights and loud audience celebrations.

And from our lofty perch, looking out across the coliseum, we see so many of our couples, all at one time, still together, enjoying each other's companionship.

We also run into them around town since Ames is only eighty thousand people. And the amazing thing is that you don't forget people with whom you went through a training that is so intimate in nature. Because when people talk openly of their issues of love, you simply don't forget them. The love relationship is very powerful, and especially so when you get down to the center of it. It's kind of sad in a way that this beautiful inner core of people's lives is so often hidden behind walls of social propriety.

As a psychologist, it is such a privilege for me to be able to work in the beautiful center of people's lives hour after hour and day after day. Each therapy hour is what I call "a universe unto itself," interesting, compelling, and truly amazing. I see clients that I worked with years ago around Ames and not only do I remember them as if it was yesterday, but I remember the issues they were working on. Why? Because being close to the inner self of people is healing, energizing, and very powerful. That's why when people are open to their inner selves, and can share that with their life partners, love thrives.

Besides working through childhood pain and trauma, much of therapy is helping people open up to their inner selves, so they can be close to their partners, their children, and their friends. And that's what children need from their parents. The parenting skills that I have outlined in this book are using that openness to talk with children rather than control and discipline. Honest sharing of feelings changes behavior in children, behavior that needs to be changed. And the behavior change is far more effective than scolding, ordering and punishing. And it keeps parents and children close rather than hurting and distancing. And kids retain their self-esteem. And they keep on loving their parents throughout their lives. Charles didn't get parents with these skills. His loving potential was lost.

Mid-Life: The Opportunity To Be Yourself

(Author: Jan) Midlife can be a more fun and satisfying stage of life than any previous time. The love and excitement of life, of course, runs through all the stages of life. It seems to be built into nature itself. The majority of people crave living and doing whatever they can to get as much living as possible. Most people dread the idea of terminal illness and the cessation of their individual existence. Most people come to accept that their mortality is inevitable, and they can't avoid leaving this world, but they don't exactly like leaving the fascinating and exciting side of being alive.

But while the earlier stages of life require a lot of attention to learning to cope, getting a vocation, having children (unless they are childless) and seeing children into adulthood, midlife finally brings the first opportunity for them to find their true selves. Childless individuals or couples can be about this stage earlier in their lives. If people are financially set up and secure, and if they can tear away from work identities, time can open up to the freedom to enjoy each day. It's a time to create and explore, and to discover and express who they truly are.

Maximum satisfaction can come in the mid-years if people make this their number one drive. It's easy to make other things primary and wonder later where the time went. People need to clarify what is most important and set limits on their culture. There is always a universe of demands that can take people away from their own centers. The end stages of life can bring a sense of lost opportunity and the awareness that the essence of life was missed somehow. People can stay busy and use up their time in lots of diversions and distractions at this stage of life, and then wake up only too late and wonder what happened. Letting death come can be a lot easier if there is a feeling that earlier stages were meaningful and fulfilling.

Were your days experienced fully and well? If there is a sense that time was used maximally and your head was in the right place at the right time, moving on feels right and OK.

People who are tuned into their deeper selves will naturally gravitate to their interests and abilities at this freer stage of life. If tuned into their selves, people have built-in sets of talents, appreciations and interests. Earlier stages of life require the development of certain abilities in order to make a living for survival. People who pay attention to these inner qualities when carving out a career will be happier and more satisfied, throughout the days of their work lives. Similarly, people who pay attention to their inner selves will also navigate midlife by paying attention to the broader interests and abilities that earlier stages of life did not allow time to develop and explore.

The question to answer in midlife is: "What do I enjoy doing?" Making a list is a way to start to become aware. For many people in the American culture, the six weeks following the New Year is the most likely time they will take the time to look at this issue each year. The question can be asked at this time, "What will I do with this year? Is what I've been doing with my time all that I want to continue to do, or is there something I might subtract or add?" How much of what I do out of obligation is legitimate and necessary, and how much of it could be reduced to free up time for what I enjoy?

Charles' retirement years do not result in this natural time for self discovery. His reliance on chemical highs and his struggle with depression has long sense diverted his attention away from healthy discovery of his talents and interests. His is a loss of human potential. His retirement years are shortened by disease. Charles doesn't get this love and joy stage in life. If his parents had received parenting skill training his life could have had a better story with a better ending.

Retirement Allows For What We Seek Most In Life - Freedom, Creativity, Companionship, Solitude

(Author: Jan) Retirement allows for what we seek in life. A marriage relationship is for love, warm companionship, fun, sexual expression, and for survival. It's for getting and eating food. It's for emotional support. Someone is always there to talk about everything that goes on in your life. In getting older, marriage is about helping one another with medical challenges.

It is also for raising kids and grandkids. Parenting and grand parenting are major talking subjects between married individuals. Two people buy a home or several homes together over a lifetime. A certain amount of time goes into taking care of houses and yards. The marriage is about each other's survival and care. You assist one another when either is ill. If you have had children together a couple can travel together to visit kids and grandkids. It's a relationship where together they can travel to see the country and the world. People need to be comfortable with, and like, their married choice to be maximally happy if they are in a relationship. This is the primary relationship. This is not saying single people have to have a love relationship to be happy. It's just saying how important healthy relationships are. Unhealthy relationships are not an asset.

For psychologically healthy people there is a second major need beyond marriage. That is to find a close friend whom you feel is a really nice person and develop a close talking relationship. This is for just being a little closer to someone else as well as the marital partner. Sometimes people have two or more such friends. These are the closer and more deeply held relationships.

These relationships are pursued in part in lieu of so many people you find - like Charles - who want to be your friend and take your time, who are needy and self centered. They have never taken responsibility for their problems. They could resolve such negative traits, but do not put themselves through the feedback from others it would take to change. I do not spend precious time with these people. Their spirits are negative. They usually are so critical of others. They would suck you dry and damage your spirit rather than be a resource of love, kindness, and joy.

Besides our relationships, there are mastery kinds of challenges to enjoy:

(Dan: age sixty eight) I spend some of my time with people who, like me, love to work up great songs, record them and perform them. Just the sheer joy of creating music is one thing - it's one of those things that simply bring joy. Humans have brains that can memorize and recall enormous amounts of words, and melodies, and harmonies. It's fun to record what we work up, and listen to it on the car CD player. It's also a great adventure to take off with a group of friends to do a show for some group of people either locally, or off across the state somewhere. Doing music either for working up songs in practice or performing for crowds is usually a mountain top experience. It puts us in direct touch with the precious creative process of the universe and life.

Retirement affords time also for other forms of creativity, the individual creativity. In retirement I find myself coveting time to be in solitude. I love the peaceful life of retirement. I love time alone with myself, and especially with my "inborn" creative abilities. I love to write. I marvel at what comes up when I sit down to write my thoughts about life and its meaning. I like to read really good books. Recently I've taken a watercolor painting class with the college of seniors. To have time to pursue a lifelong desire to draw and paint is a pure delight.

It's a lot of fun to feel the learning curve that takes place in learning something entirely new.

I also love to work with family pictures, and to catch Kodak moments both of my kids and grandkids. I like to catch that "moment for ever" when it happens. That can be of the beauty in nature or man's accomplishments like bridges, barns and places beautifully planted and groomed by man.

Beyond all this, one of my greatest joys is reactivating the machinery handling skills of my farm youth. I had my uncle's old favorite 1958 Power Master Ford Tractor restored, inside and out. Now I can mow our beautiful pasture floor along the creek amongst the timber below our home. I can disc up sod when the neighbor or I want to open up some timber and reshape our lawns on down into the pasture below. I can spend hours working down behind my house whether on my big tractor, or on my lawn tractor, for all kinds of aesthetic improvements of our property. I'm totally at peace down there. Uncle Jerry was a farmer, so as a kid I enjoyed the farm. The power of the machines together with the childhood and youth skills of handling them is another great enjoyment in my retired life.

My motorcycle presents another learning curve for skills that I had never had in my life before. It's about freedom. It's simply there for when a great sunrise or sunset is taking place. When the conditions are right, there is nothing like the free feeling of moving out into the exhilarating air. I can smell the fields. I can enjoy the beauty of a powerful and graceful machine as color fills the sky. Another of the joys of cycling is the "lost days" out in the world. Either alone or with friends, I can choose each turn as the spirit moves me - pure freedom. It's wonderful.

All of the above experiences, as I think about it, may be means of experiencing the God who may be there, just beyond the pale. All are ways of experiencing the creative and beautiful forces of life. And when I'm in tune with life's love of fun and creativity, I'm being. It may be why I'm here.

(Author: Jan) Carl Jung[16] was the other famous psychiatrist along with Sigmund Freud who worked in the early twentieth

---

16 Carl Jung. Two Essays on Analytical Psychology. Princeton University Press, 1953.

century. Unlike Freud, Jung believed God was real. Both Jung and Martin Buber believed that when people exercised their creativity, they were expressing the God of the universe. I have always liked this notion.

If our lives have gone well, our elder years can be a time of maximum creativity in whatever ways we are creative. It's also a time of maximum fulfillment of love capability. We can be free full time to love our partners, our parents, our kids, our grandkids, our friends and neighbors, our world, it seems. We can be a beacon of light unto the world at this stage of our lives. Love can be in every touch, in every family meal, in every gathering of friends.

It's a time of life to be fully content and satisfied. We no longer need to feel love hunger. We are no longer giving ourselves away through constant work and raising kids. It is a time of receiving to full satisfaction. (Again, childless couples may get a head start on this stage.) It's a time when we can feel fully loved. It's a time to feel deeper. It's a time to be more aware of all our surroundings and everything good in life. It's a time to be aware of the value of each person, of all good relationships, of nature, of friendships, and of all the love in our environment. It's a time to better communicate love. It's a time to feel a part of something bigger than the self. It's a time to affirm the world and universe we live in, and it's a time to be no longer afraid of death.

(Dan: age seventy five) Charles, on the other hand, drinks alone. When he got to retirement age and left his work, he found himself alone in life. He returned to drinking in an attempt to feel better. All he had on his schedule was worship and a Tuesday church class. In an attempt to fill the emptiness and lack of relationships, he fell off the wagon. He'd appear at church disheveled and inebriated.

Twice in his retired years his church put him into treatment. But after a few months, each time he slipped away from sobriety. Charles died of liver failure while still a young retiree. I was at his side on the day he died. None of his family appeared that day. Later I learned his son was out on the golf course near-by.

I thought of all of Charles' potential. I remembered his cleverness as a child and his hope for his future. He had the same playfulness and love for life of any of us. I thought of Grandpa's words that much suffering will continue until society incorporates the psychological wisdom of the last few centuries. Charles told me that his only hope was for "a forgiving God who might remember a hopeless sinner". He said his life "felt like a museum of lost opportunities". He died a troubled and unsatisfied soul.

The Last Days: Peace, Love, Fulfilment. Prepare For Blast Off

(Dan: age ninety three) Years later in my early nineties, I lay in my own death bed. My wife and kids keep vigil by my side. I have timed my recent days and weeks so as to ask people to come spend some time with me. I couldn't move well anymore, but my spirit was alive with interest, curiosity about death, and a love of so many with whom I wanted to have some conversations before I was gone.

The love I gathered into myself in those last weeks was incredible. I had so many relationships with people, some very close, some far away, but so many who were willing to come to be with me in my final hours. No matter the distance in geography, I had untold numbers of old friends that life's path had shared along the way. Distance and time had not dampened the love in those relationships one bit.

I knew I was shrouded in love. Final conversations were simply to celebrate and enjoy once more those old connections. Just being with one another, felt good. Human love is an amazing thing. I have felt supported throughout my life wherever I went. If God is universal love, then he had come to me through the hugs and kisses and conversations of a lifetime. He came through different arms and faces in different times and places, but He was always there.

I have lived my life fully. I have laughed and cried with loved ones. I have seen the world in so many amazing places. I have had a challenging, fascinating, and loving career. I followed my beloved grandpa into psychology to be close to people in my work and to make a difference in peoples' lives. In my work I loved so many people striving to live better.

I have had a loving wife who has always been with me since that day in the library. She has been there for me throughout my terminal illness, caring so beautifully and so well, through every challenging moment. I would wish I could do the same for her, but I have the satisfaction of knowing my children were well loved and cared for growing up in our family, and they will be there for her all the way.

When children are loved well, they love back. Of all the things that children are for people, they are truly protection in our old age. If we are in nursing care, they advocate for us. If we can't hear, they get next to our good ear and have close-up conversations. If we can't see well, they watch carefully for us as we go around corners or down steps. If we can't walk well, they are by our side to keep us from falling. If we are in wheel chairs, they haul us to bleachers, stadiums, little league games, graduations, baby showers and weddings. They keep us connected with friends and family. When we try to thank them for their care and attentiveness, they shrug it off, saying, "they can never in a life time pay us back for our giving them life, and caring for them for eighteen years."

My kids, my grandkids, and my great grandkids have streamed through my life in these most recent months. They bring gifts of conversations about their lives and all the exciting things they are doing. They bring tokens of their love: pictures, handmade gifts, poems and even a tiny live frog.

When we have the skills to love well, we are loved well in return. Death is not really unwelcome, as my body finally gives over to life's years of loving and enjoying. My heart is full beyond belief. I was given full permission early on in life to live to my full potential. Life has been fun, exciting and fulfilling from birth to death. I could not have lived more fully. I filled every minute with my maximum capacity to enjoy, to love, and to be loved.

I take my partner's hand. I take my child's hand. I let go into total confidence and trust. Most likely, a world so beautiful and a life lived so well can only be evidence of more to come. Here I go. Let's see what's next. Is that my mother's heart beat I hear above me? Thump, Thump, Thump. I'm not sure what it is, but I like it.

Conclusions

Relationship skills can make huge differences in how people's lives go and end up. Horace Mann envisioned the importance of universal education for democracy to work. It would be good to see skill training for relationships made universal in schools, colleges, churches and in communities in order to bring about the vision of this book.

School counselors are already highly trained in relationship skills. Colleges have psychologists and social workers in their counseling centers. Community mental health centers have similar professionals. Many churches have graduate trained pastoral counselors already capable of giving this training. These professionals are loaded up doing treatment of mental patients. We need more of them for prevention work, namely skill training for normal people.

If a small part of the new money coming for the improvement of mental health in this country could go toward educating more mental health professionals a cadre of professionals could be financed to provide skill training. With widespread skill training, the United States could become a better place. The second requirement would be for schools and colleges to get skill training onto their curricula. Now is prime time for getting institutions on board for this program. The whole country is aware of the need and searching for answers. If the United States adopted human relations skill training on a large scale basis, many countries would soon follow. It's common for democratic countries, developed and underdeveloped, to follow the United States in ways of improving civilization.

Since mass shootings have become practically daily events in our culture, both Republican and Democrat politicians have become motivated to put money into mental health. Some great ideas have been incorporated into the Mental Health Reform Act of 2016 for getting early intervention into the lives of mentally ill citizens to help prevent homicides.

To help train up a cadre of professionals to do universal skill training like what I have outlined in this book would cost a small portion of what the United States pays in a year for mental health treatment. I'm hoping my book can find its way into Congress, into seminary education, and onto college campuses and into local mental health centers.

The Positive Psychology class at Harvard is a model now for colleges to emulate. A skill training class requirement in college curriculums could go a long way toward improving college educated Americans' lives. It could bring happiness and fulfillment to people's lives and prevent enormous mental suffering and medical expense. It's been established that when people have less stress in their lives, they are more disease free and live longer.

Tele behavioral health through use of computer screens is receiving good financing by the Mental Health Reform Act of 2016, which will allow for people in remote underserved areas to get immediate psychological services. Skill training could be provided by computer screen throughout the country, aiding locally trained professionals to apply the training face to face to citizens, students and parishioners. The technology is here. The time is right. Great strides can be accomplished.

I have a dream. I have a dream for one giant psychological leap for humankind.

About the Author

Jan Dale is a retired psychologist. He was raised on a farm in Iowa. His ability to connect with people was seen as early as his elementary and adolescent years. His love of people and community was seen when he was a paper boy for seven years in Brooklyn, Iowa. In high school, he served as president of both Iowa 4-H and South Iowa Methodist Youth. In college, his junior year he served as Vice-President of the Simpson College student body in Indianola, Iowa, and studied political science at American University in Washington D.C. his senior year. The focus in Washington D.C. was international relations.

He earned his Ph.D. from Boston University in 1971. While working on his Ph.D., he spent one year in clinical training at the Harvard Teaching Hospital for psychiatrists, Massachusetts Mental Health Center. His Ph.D. at Boston University was interdisciplinary. It was a five year Ph.D. It equipped him as a licensed psychologist, but provided two additional years in the Psychology of Religion. He worked for Arthur D. Little, a management consultant firm in Cambridge, Massachusetts, for two years while working on his Ph.D. He was a Research Consultant for Arthur D. Little. His work was to research and coordinate ecumenical cooperation of seminary presidents and deans in the Chicago area.

He completed his Ph.D. in 1971, and took the position of Chief Psychologist for the Central Iowa Mental Health Center in Ames, Iowa. He loved developmental psychology and relationship psychology and wanted to work with all age groups, couples, and families. His Ph.D. had emphasized prevention as well as treatment, and this job allowed him to work half time in prevention and half time in treatment.

He taught skill training in prevention workshops for twenty years in areas of couple communication, healthy parenting, parenting for healthy adolescent sexual development, and stress management. He was the psychological consultant to both the adolescent drug treatment program, Youth and Shelter Services and the residential children's treatment program in Ames, Iowa, Beloit of Iowa. He served both programs for ten years each. Dr. Dale received awards from the Guidance Counselors Association of Central Iowa for "Outstanding Contributions to Youth," and from the Community Mental Health Association of Iowa for "For His Work as a Therapist, Consultant, and Educator".

This book is about preventing psychological suffering, and enhancing psychologically healthy relationships; it's also about achieving happiness and fulfillment through all the stages of life. It's a book to help normal people succeed in love relationships. It's to help people have loving marriages and to raise happy and healthy kids.

He met his wife Donna in college. She became an elementary teacher. Together they have raised three happy, healthy and competent kids, now themselves parents of middle school and elementary aged kids. Two of his children have taken spouses who were born on other continents. In this book Jan presents listening, conflict resolution and value communication skills that protect and maintain the natural love feelings. Protecting and maintaining natural love feelings can lead to greater success and cooperation in all areas of life: home, business, industry, religion, government and amongst the nations.

Jan followed a History and Political Science major at Simpson College with a minister's degree at Boston University School of Theology and a master's equivalent in the core clinical psychology program at Boston University graduating in 1966. Boston University was the seminary that Martin Luther King Jr. attended eight years earlier. Dr. Dale worked for five years as a minister of a United Congregational Church, and a United Methodist Church during seminary and in early stages of his Ph.D. studies. His purpose in writing this book is to help pull the world along towards psychologically happier and healthier children and adults. He wants the skills presented in this book to also prepare the world for less hostile international and religious conflict.